Secrets

of the

Notch

Secrets of the Notch

*A Guide to Rock and Ice Climbing
in Franconia Notch State Park
and surrounding areas*

by

Jon Sykes

Huntington Graphics
Burlington, Vermont

First Edition, 2001
Copyright 2001, Huntington Graphics, all rights reserved
Printed in Canada

Publisher: Huntington Graphics
            P.O. Box 373
            Burlington, VT 05402

ISBN 1-886064-13-X, includes index

Layout, design and maps: John Hadden, Resting Lion Studio
Maps for the Lincoln area: Brian Whitfield
Map of Franconia Notch: Eric Pospesil

Editing: Jason Evans, Jared Gange, and Linda Young
Project assistance: Laurie Caswell Burke

Photographers as credited
Cover photo: Chris Marks leading The Late Show on Eagle Cliff
Photographer: Jamie Cunningham
Back cover photo: Art Mooney leading Hollow Hell at Echo Crag
Photographer: Eric Pospesil

The Old Man of the Mountain   Jamie Fitz

"Men hang out their signs indicative of their respective trades. Shoemakers hang out a gigantic shoe; jewelers, a monster watch; even a dentist hangs out a gold tooth; but in the Franconia Mountains God Almighty has hung out a sign to show that in New England He makes men."

Daniel Webster, 1831

Acknowledgments

A special thanks is necessary to the many people past and present for their contribution to the writing of the guide books of the past, and to the making of this guide, the most comprehensive climbing guide ever written for this historic area. Without the documentation of the many routes over the last 81 years, none of what you read now would be possible. Thanks go to Howard Peterson for the first guide (**Cannon, A Climber's Guide**, 1972 and 1975), Paul Ross and Chris Ellms for their 1978 guide (**Cannon, Cathedral, Humphrey's and Whitehorse, A Rock Climber's Guide**), and of course to Ed Webster for his 1982 and 1986 editions of **Rock Climbs in the White Mountains of New Hampshire**.

To follow in the footsteps of such men is a daunting task that I now fully appreciate, having written my own book. Below is a list of the many people involved either directly or indirectly with this guide. Andy Tuthill, Susan Frankenstein, Chris Ellms, Jed Eliades, Stoney Middleton, Jamie Cunningham, Doug Teschner, Rick Wilcox, Jim Shimberg, Paul Cormier, Chris Marks, Gareth Slattery, Eric and Ajilla Pospesil, Brad White, Tom Callaghan, Tom Nonnis, Paul (Base) Boissonneault, Henry and Jill Barber, Ted Hammond, Roger Martin, Chris Rowins, Steve Schneider, Steve Dupuis, Tom Lyman, Al Rubin, Mike Lee, Alan Pilgrim, Peter Henden, Bill Keiler, Lois LaRock, Eric Carpenter, Tim Kemple Sr., Tim Kemple Jr., Shad and Janel Lawton, Brian Whitfield, Chuck Woodman, Kai Poesse, Joe TerraVecchia, Karin Bates, and, of course, Ed Webster for his help in documenting Echo Crag in 1996. And a special thanks goes to Rick Wilcox and Nick Yardley for looking over the manuscript in its final stages.

A personal thanks needs to be made to all the people who have helped me in the pursuit of my chosen craft. Many friends have either let me sleep on their floor or allowed me the use of a spare room for months at a time, not to mention the use of various driveways and parcels of land on which to camp. For ten years my friends have tolerated my nomadic lifestyle, allowing me to be the climber I am today. I owe everything to them: Gareth and Nicole Slattery for opening up their home and family to me for many years; Lucy Wyman and Craig Harmon for their "come-on-in-if-we-can-fit-you" policy and enduring friendship; Mike Lee for his floor space and for being one of the bubbas; Chris Marks for being strong when I have been weak; and his wife Caren for her sharp north country wit; Bill and Michelle

Rzepa for allowing me to camp on their land; Chuck Woodman for showing me the way to the world of climbing; and Eric Pospesil for his intense drive and desire to learn the true excitement of ground-up first ascents. Jared Gange, my publisher, has shown great patience in dealing with my lack of writing skills and literary ineptness. He has become a friend and confidant. Thanks to Gardner Kellogg of Kellogg Surveying and Mapping in Littleton for putting me to work off and on, and for the use of a rotary hammer drill for replacing old bolts on Cannon and elsewhere. Jim Lindorf for being a friend to me and opening up his heart and home to me many times. A very special thanks goes to Jamie Cunningham for devoting so much time and money to photographing the Notch and the many climbers who grace these pages. A special thanks to John Hadden of Resting Lion Studio for his computer wizardry and infinite patience. And to my family for their support all these years, I love you. The list could go on and on forever, for I have been blessed by kindness and compassion from many people throughout the years, and I thank you all.

The Friends of Franconia Notch is a newly organized non-profit coalition of climbers and hikers interested in the preservation of the Notch's many trails and cliffs.

Our goal is simple: To organize and carry out yearly trail clean-up days and annual cliff clean-up days. What does this mean to you, the climber? Due to the increase in the popularity of climbing, trails are eroding at an alarming rate with the increase in traffic. If we use the trails, then we must help with maintaining them. We also have an obligation as climbers to replace old rusted pitons and bolts on the many cliffs throughout the White Mountains. The Friends of Franconia Notch already has begun both by doing major trail work in the Notch as well as replacing many bolts on Cannon and elsewhere. While the labor is free, the bolts and pins are not. We understand that many climbers who live out-of-state are here only for a brief visit and only have time to climb. If you can't help out in person, then your financial support is the next best thing.

It is also our goal to create a local fast response high-angle rescue team to ensure faster, possibly life-saving rescues on Cannon and elsewhere. The Friends are also committed to the installment of a much-needed privy at the climber parking lot. With your support everyone can enjoy Franconia Notch for a long time to come. The Friends can be reached by accessing their website at **www.friendsnotch.org.** A percentage of the profits from this book will go to The Friends of Franconia Notch, to be used towards various on-going projects within the Notch.

Table of Contents

Introduction

Soaring high above the valley floor of Franconia Notch is one of the greatest granite walls in the eastern United States. Cannon Cliff captured my imagination back in the 1970s, but it was not until the early 1980s that a local climber named Chuck Woodman asked if I would rock climb with him. For the next four years we climbed together, and Chuck introduced me to the wonders of Cannon's mythical flanks. What began as another wild sport for me to dabble in became my life's work. Franconia Notch is my home, its walls my sanctuary. No other place in the East will command your attention more than the Notch.

The purpose of this guide book is to inform and enlighten the climbing community of the wealth of rock, ice, and mixed climbing routes in and around the Notch. Steeped in a strong tradition dating back to 1919 when a mixed snow and ice route was ascended just to the right of Lakeview, the Notch has become a proving ground for some of the finest climbers in the country.

The 1990s saw a period of rebirth of exploration and when the dust settled, over 200 new routes of all kinds had been recorded. The majority of new routes are on the eastern side of the parkway. Cannon and the Eaglet are no longer the sole destinations. Now included are: Artist's Bluff, Echo Crag, Profile Cliff, and Hound's Hump Ridge, which includes Split Rock, the Wing, the Flatiron, Long Wall, Gully Wall, and of course, Eagle Cliff and Lafayette Ledges. Indian Head, Lincoln Crag and Potash Knob in Lincoln also have been added to the list of places to climb.

How to use this guide book: A cliff and route index can be found in the back of the book. You will find each cliff or crag title on the page headings throughout the book.

Maps: The maps to each crag or cliff system can be found at the start of each cliff description.

Regulations: Franconia Notch State Park is under the management of the New Hampshire Department of Resources and Economic Development, Division of Parks and Recreation. NH Division of Parks does not regulate climbing in any way. That means it's up to us, the climbing community, to regulate, manage, and maintain a minimum impact philosophy within the Notch and throughout our world.

Climbers should take out the trash they carry in, and pick up any left behind from thoughtless misusers of our Mother Earth. They should stay on existing, developed trails while hiking and dispose of human waste by digging a six-inch deep hole at least 200 feet from water and bury the waste. Recreational users should pack out toilet paper in a ziplock bag, or better yet, use dried leaves that will break down naturally. Please use discretion when placing bolts and fixing protection in the White Mountains and respect seasonal cliff closures that protect nesting birds of prey.

Explanation of map to right:

The map of the Franconia Notch State Park area on the right shows the key features of interest to climbers. Approaching from the south on Interstate 93, Cannon Cliff is the dominant feature on your left, and the various outcroppings of Hound's Hump Ridge appear straight ahead. New Hampshire's famous landmark and state symbol, The Old Man of the Mountain, is at the northern end of Cannon Cliff, above Profile Lake. Cannon Ski Area and its tramway are just beyond on the left. As you drive pass Echo Lake, you will see the low cliff known as Artist's Bluff ahead and to your left.

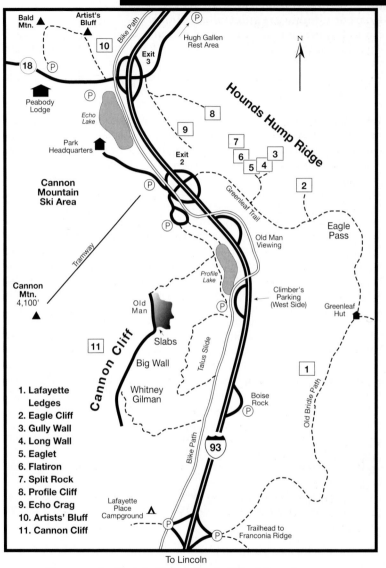

Bald Mtn.

Artist's Bluff

Bike Path

10

Exit 3

P

Hugh Gallen Rest Area

N

18 P

Peabody Lodge

P

Echo Lake

Park Headquarters

8

9

Hounds Hump Ridge

Cannon Mountain Ski Area

Exit 2

7

6 3

5 4

P

Greenleaf Trail

2

Eagle Pass

Tramway

P

Old Man Viewing

Cannon Mtn. 4,100'

Profile Lake

Climber's Parking (West Side)

Greenleaf Hut

Old Man

Slabs

11

Cannon Cliff

Big Wall

Whitney Gilman

Talus Slide

P

1

Old Bridle Path

Boise Rock

P

1. Lafayette Ledges
2. Eagle Cliff
3. Gully Wall
4. Long Wall
5. Eaglet
6. Flatiron
7. Split Rock
8. Profile Cliff
9. Echo Crag
10. Artists' Bluff
11. Cannon Cliff

Bike Path

93

Lafayette Place Campground

P

P

Trailhead to Franconia Ridge

To Lincoln

Franconia Notch State Park Climbing Areas

Current climbing regulations include:

No rock climbing in state-protected peregrine falcon nesting areas from April 1st until the end of July. Please look for and abide by all posted signs in peregrine sensitive areas. In addition, cliff closure lists are posted at local climbing shops each spring. No camping or fires are allowed on state or National Forest land that has been posted.

Registration: Signing in and out for rock climbs on Cannon Cliff is very important, particularly for first-time Cannon climbers. It ensures that if an emergency should arise, someone other than your partner knows where you are and can take the necessary steps for a safe rescue, if needed.

Rescue: New Hampshire Fish and Game is the first line of defense in any rescue situation. Before a rescue starts, Fish and Game must be notified. The best way to contact them is through New Hampshire State Police in Twin Mountain. After being contacted about a potential rescue situation, Fish and Game will then call upon either Mountain Rescue Services, Inc. or Androscoggin Valley Search and Rescue. Mountain Rescue Service, Inc. is based out of International Mountain Equipment (IME) in North Conway, NH, and is run by local climbers on a volunteer basis. These climbers are trained in high-angle rescue, as well as wilderness first aid and mountain rescue. Androscoggin Valley Search and Rescue, AVSAR for short, based out of Randolph, NH, does not perform high-angle rescues, but does help with carry outs and is very proficient at finding lost or hurt people.

Franconia Notch has some of the most difficult and committing climbs in the East, yet there is no high-angle rescue team as of this writing for this extensive alpine area. It is the goal of the Friends of Franconia Notch to raise money through the sale of this book and private donations to train a team of locals in high-angle rescue. With the continual growth of our sport it is inevitable that more accidents will occur.

In case of an accident while climbing in the White Mountains, call as directed below:

NH State Police, F Troop, Twin Mountain 603-846-3333
NH Fish and Game: call the State Police (above) to have your call directed to an on-duty officer
911 calls are routed to NH State Police
From cell phones, call ∗77

The use of cell phones in the White Mountains is less than reliable. And the misuse of a cell phone (such as unnecessary calls for rescue) can put others in grave danger. For example, don't call for a rescue if you are on Lunch Ledge and night rolls in. While carrying a cell phone is now common practice, this should in no way replace good judgement and adequate preparation especially on the longer or more difficult routes.

The Climber Registration box at the climber parking lot near the base of Cannon Cliff.

Free Climbing Ratings

An approximate comparison of the three most widely recognized international rating systems follows.

American	French	British
5.0		Difficult
5.1		
5.2		Very Difficult
5.3		Severe
5.4		
5.5		
5.6	3	
5.7	3+	Very Severe
5.8	4+	Hard Very Severe
5.9	5	
5.9+	5+	E1
5.10a	6a	
5.10b	6a	E2
5.10c	6a+	
5.10d	6b	E3
5.11a	6b+	
5.11a	6c	E4
5.11b	6c+	
5.11c	7a	
5.11d	7a	E5
5.12a	7a+	
5.12b	7b	
5.12c	7b+	E6
5.12d	7c	
5.13a	7c+	
5.13b	8a	E7
5.13c	8a+	
5.13d	8b	E8
5.14a	8b+	
5.14b	8c	E9
5.14c	8c+	
5.14d	9a	E10

Artificial (Aid) Climbing Ratings

A0 Resting on protection while free climbing, or a tension traverse, pendulum, or rappeling on a traversing or diagonal route.

A1 Direct aid on well-placed protection: nuts, cams, pitons, or bolts.

A2 Difficult and sometimes awkward protection, such as micro nuts, shallow or flaring cam placements, and/or tied-off pitons interspersed with good protection.

A3 Much more delicate than A2, requiring stacking pins and/or rurps, peckers, bird beaks, hooking and whatever else you can conjure up.

A4 Body weight placements with at least a 40-foot fall factor.

A5 Body-weight placements with greater than a 60-foot fall factor and with the potential for serious injury.

The **C rating** (C1, C2, etc.) stands for clean aid—without the use of hammer or pitons; wire nuts and cams only.

The **M rating** is for mixed rock and ice. It runs from M1 to M10, where M5 corresponds to 5.9, M6 to 5.10, etc., up and down the Class 5 scale.

★ Star Rating

For those who are new to the sport, a star placed next to a route title indicates this is a great route. No star means the route is of average interest. In the past, a more complicated three star rating system was used to differentiate among good, great, and classic routes.

In this guide book, we do away with the three stars and use just one star, indicating that this is a great climb. For years, many people would climb the three-star routes only, creating an overcrowding problem, which in turn led to more injuries from rock fall. The one star rating system will hopefully relieve some of the overcrowding and encourage climbers to sample many other great routes.

Protection Ratings

The letters R (runout) and X (extreme) are used in this book to indicate protection quality. The R rating represents a route with runouts and/or poor protection, with falls usually no longer than 30 or 40 feet. The X rating represents the universal sign of death: extreme danger of hitting the ground with very little, if any, protection to stop or even slow a person down. If there is no R or X rating given, then one can assume the climb in question has reasonable protection, bearing in mind that conditions (including protection) do change.

General Comments

Route descriptions are your key to success, but they also can lead down the road to failure. The purpose of a guide book is to give you, the climber, detailed information on each area and each climb. But too much information takes away a piece of the adventure. It is my desire to put something back into the adventure and joys of route finding. This book is detailed, yet you will find that I don't give complete details on gear selection, or techniques for climbing roofs, dihedrals, cracks, slabs, etc. You can find these things in how-to-climb books. This guide book will get you to the cliff and to the climb and give you details about the climb, but you, the climber, are responsible for ascending it safely.

At the base of Old Cannon, now known as the Zone:

The author standing in the "zone of destruction" one week after one of the largest rockslides in Cannon's history.   Chris Marks

Personal Note

When I first decided to write this guide book, I had no idea what a can of worms I was opening. In particular, I found that the route descriptions for some of the old routes were far from correct. Also, new route descriptions that had been documented in a ledger in IME's retail store in North Conway had inexplicably vanished, making my task that much more difficult. There always will be something written incorrectly or credit given to the wrong person or persons. I have made every effort to provide the climbing community with a guide book that is free of errors and omissions, however, as anyone who has ever written a book will agree, some things inevitably fall through the cracks. This is where you, the climber, come into play. With your help we can correct any erroneous route descriptions or other errors to make the best climbing guide possible.

Below is my mailing address, so that you may send any corrections to me. Any comments about the guide book or opinions are greatly appreciated.

It has been an honor to be part of the continuing exploration of the Notch and its surrounding crags. I hope that you will enjoy and respect it here as much as I and the others who help maintain this incredible place.

Thanks,

Jon M. Sykes

Jon Sykes
P. O. Box 576
Franconia, NH 03580

This book is dedicated to my mother
and to the well-known climber & author, Guy Waterman

Cannon Cliff

September 18, 1928, the first ascent of Cannon Cliff began when Robert L. M. Underhill teamed up with Lincoln O'Brien to create New Cannon (now known as Old Cannon). These two great climbers would go on to forge new routes all over the world.

Standing nearly one thousand feet tall and over a mile wide, Cannon is perhaps the most demanding and committing alpine wall in the eastern United States. It offers classic routes such as Lakeview, Consolation Prize, Vertigo, Union Jack, Moby Grape, and, of course, the best ridge route in New Hampshire, the Whitney–Gilman. And for those who need more of a challenge, the big wall offers some of the hardest traditional climbing anywhere. Routes like the Ghost, VMC Direct, Labyrinth Wall, Benedictus Direct, and Fruit Cup Wall are some of the longest in the Northeast. There is something for everyone to enjoy on Cannon.

All fun aside, there are three major concerns to keep in mind when climbing at Cannon. The first and most important concern is loose rock and an increase in rock slides. Rockfalls have historically been a problem due to the fact that Cannon is an exfoliation dome that is peeling like the layers of an onion. Many locals, and others, have noted an increase in

Cannon Cliff, the Big Wall   Jamie Cunningham

slides over the past ten years. I attribute this to global warming. While some deny this theory, the increase in rockfall appears to be something we have to contend with now, whatever the cause.

The second cause for concern is that all fixed protection has the potential to be dubious and always should be questioned and backed up with natural protection wherever possible. Pitons and old 1/4" bolts are the greatest concern.

Last, but by no means least, climbers should respect the fact that Cannon is an east-facing wall. Thus it obstructs the view of weather systems approaching from the west. Climbers should be prepared by checking both local and national forecasts for up-to-date conditions before attempting to climb this cliff.

Cannon Cliff, as you can guess, is not a place to learn how to climb. Please be careful, and be sure to sign in at the climber registration box at the climber parking lot on the southbound side of Route 3/93 beside Profile Lake. This is the best insurance for first-time climbers. A cell phone is not the answer to survival on a cliff like Cannon. Common sense and a thorough understanding of alpine climbing will get a person a lot further.

Directions to Cannon and the approach trails

Located on the southbound side of Interstate 93 in Franconia Notch State Park, just south of Exit 2, Cannon Tram parking and Profile Lake are the trailhead parking and boat launch. The climber registration box is located at the south end of the parking lot. In the past, there were three ways to approach Cannon Cliff. Now there are only two ways to the base of the wall that are being maintained.

The first and safest route up through the immense talus slope is the **Lakeview Trail** on the north side of Cannon. Walk south past the sign-in box on the bike path, cross over the first bridge, and turn hard right (north), following a trail for a short distance to just before a narrow footbridge on your right crossing the brook. Turn left here and follow a well-defined trail up to the talus slope below the slabs. Wind your way through the boulders past small cairns until just below a tree band separating you from the cliff. Stay right and follow a path through the trees leading to the base of Lakeview, or, trend left at the trees following another path that leads to Horrifying Ear and Consolation Prize. To descend from the base of the Slabs, follow small cairns back down the talus.

The **Whitney-Gilman Trail** can be found by walking south on the bike path about a quarter mile until a trail appears on your right. You should be able to see the south end of the cliff through the woods from the bike path. Hike up until you exit through spruce scrub and onto the talus slope. To your left (south) a little ways is a large white boulder known as the Little Matterhorn. (When standing at the base of the Whitney-Gilman Ridge looking down the talus slope, you can see the distinct Little Matterhorn which tells you where the trail enters the woods. If you miss it, you will regret it.) Hike the talus past an occasional small cairn up to the Whitney-Gilman Ridge, and/or trend right to Duet and Sam's Swan Song.

Descent Routes

Descending from the top of Cannon requires a walk-off. From the top of Duet heading north all the way to Lakeview, descend via the Lakeview descent trail on top of the Old Man. Follow a man-made water trough to the start of the trail down; when you reach Profile Lake, turn right (south) and follow the trail beside the lake back to the parking lot.

Whitney-Gilman Descent Trail

From the top of the Whitney-Gilman Ridge head up, following the trail until it turns south and starts dropping down the ridge very steeply. Follow the trail down to the bike path and hike north back to the trailhead parking lot. Caution: Both trails from the top can be iced up in late fall and early spring, creating a life-threatening situation. Be extra careful during these times.

Note: Routes on Cannon Cliff are described from left to right—south to north—starting with Henderson Buttress and ending with Lakeview.

Route listings for Anderson Wall

1. Henderson II 5.5
2. Pilaf II 5.9
3. Eastern Bushido III 5.8 A4
4. The Guillotine III 5.10, A2
5. Odessa Steps I 5.9 (5.7 R)
6. Muir II 5.7 R
7. Achilles Heel III 5.10
8. Ambrosia III 5.8
9. The Whitney-Gilman Ridge II 5.7

For routes 5-8, only the climb's start is indicated, leaving something for the adventurous spirit!

John Hession

Anderson Wall south of Whitney-Gilman

Jamie Cunningham

Whitney-Gilman and the ominous Black Dike

Route listings for Cannonade to Triple S Buttress

1. Cannonade II 5.4
2. Cannonade Buttress
3. The British Were Coming IV 5.8
4. The Duet Buttress
5. Triple S Buttress

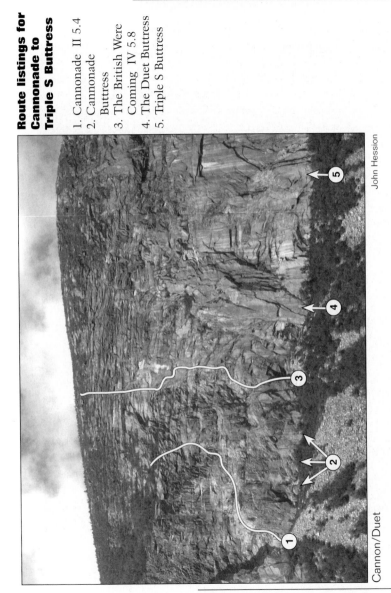

John Hession

Cannon/Duet

Cannon Big Wall

Jamie Cunningham

Route listings for Cannon Big Wall

1. The British Were Coming IV 5.8
2. Duet III 5.7
3. Slow & Easy I 5.8
4. Sticky Fingers I 5.10
5. Midlife Crisis IV 5.9 A4 (5.8 R)
6. Sam's Swan Song III 5.7
7. The Ghost and the Ghost Roof IV 5.9 A4
8. VMC Direct V 5.11
9. VMC Direct Direct IV 5.10+
10. Labyrinth Wall Direct V 5.11 (5.10 R) or (5.8 A2)
11. Benedictus Direct IV 5.11 A3

Moby Grape to Down East

Jamie Cunningham

Route listings for Moby Grape to Down East

1. YMC Dike IV 5.10 R
2. Moby Grape III 5.8 with alternate Reppy's Crack start
   and Kurt's Corner finish shown in dashed lines.
3. The Dolomite Wall III 5.10
4. Union Jack III 5.9
5. Vertigo III 5.9 R A0
6. White Iceberg III 5.12a
7. Down East III 5.10a R

John Hession

The Zone Area, with Cannon Slabs to the right and Vertigo to the left

Route listings for The Zone & Cannon Slabs

1. Whale Watchers II 5.9 (5.7 R)
2. Old Cannon III 5.6

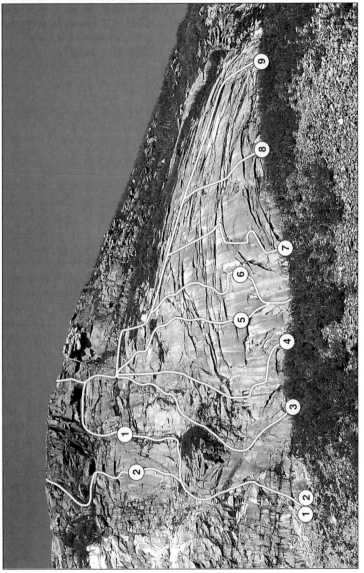

Jamie Cunningham

The Slabs

Route listings for The Slabs

1. Wiessner's Buttress III 5.6
2. Riddler III 5.9
3. Wiessner's Dike III 5.6
4. Falling Aspirations III 5.9
5. Odyssey of an Artichoke III 5.10
6. Consolation Prize III 5.8
7. Vendetta II 5.9
8. The Hold II 5.9+
9. Lakeview II 5.5 (with Wiessner's Buttress finish, 5.6)

Henderson Buttress Area

Henderson II 5.5

The start is on the north side (right) of the Henderson Buttress.

1. Traverse left from north to the east-facing front of the buttress. Climb up broken rock to a ledge. 130', 5.2
2. From ledge, traverse left to a meadow. 140', 5.4
3. Climb left twenty feet, ascend a groove to trees. 110', 5.5
4. Move right through bushes to slabs and a short wall. 130', 5.5
5. Climb crack in a short pillar, gain a tree ledge, traverse right twenty feet around a nose to the top. 100', 5.4

FA: Kenneth Henderson, Robert Bates, William House, Betty Woolsey, Henry Baldwin, and Robert Bishop September 29, 1940

Noonie Direct II 5.7

Start at the base of Henderson Buttress on the right side.

1. Face climb up fifty feet (5.3) to easy terrain, joining Henderson. 130', 5.3
2. Climb broken rock to grass platform. Henderson goes left, and you ascend straight up thirty feet, traverse fifteen feet left, past a bulge, belay on grassy alcove below a corner. 110', 5.7
3. Climb steep open book for twenty feet, step onto right hand wall at a sloping stance, use a flake to reach large, sloping alcove under an overhang. 40', 5.6
4. Climb onto outside face of buttress, ascend corner to a jam crack in another inside corner, follow this twenty feet, surmount a left-facing overhang. Step right, then diagonally right through broken rock to bushes. 100', 5.7
5. Climb detached block on right to a ledge and trees.

FA: Joe LaBelle, Pay Hoyt, Howard Stidham, and Jack Ragle July 22, 1967

Variation: High Noon Crack I 5.8

3a. Jam the fist-to-finger crack in the open book to the top. 5.8

FA: Dave Anderson and Jim Fitzpatrick August 18, 1982

★ Pilaf II 5.9

Pilaf is the striking crack high on the north wall of Henderson Buttress.

1. The climb starts up Henderson heading up a thirty foot wall to bushes and follows a diagonal line right on loose blocks across the north wall to the start of the hand crack. 150', 5.9

Mike Lee seconding the first ascent of Eastern Bushido   Jon Sykes

2. Jam and layback up the steep hand crack to ledges on Henderson Buttress. Either climb Henderson to the top or rappel with two ropes to the ground.

History: Mark Whitton and Tad Pheffer led the crux upper crack in June, 1976. One week later, while leading the second ascent, Stoney Middleton and Andy Tuthill added a harder direct start, mentioned above.

The Anderson Wall

Eastern Bushido   III 5.8 A4 (5.6 R)

This route starts fifty feet right of the north wall of Henderson Buttress and in my opinion is one of the more frightening loose climbs on Cannon. The first pitch had been climbed previously but no information is known as to the ascentist.

1. Ascend easy ground (5.2) up to a right facing corner (50'). A lone 1/4" bolt (old) was found here. Free climb right of bolt up broken ramp to left-facing shallow corner, up this free or aid past loose flakes to the top of a large ledge and a two-bolt belay. (A lone 1½" angle piton and 11mm piece of climbing rope were found here.) 140', 5.8 A2 (loose)

2. Follow ramp up and right ten feet, then straight up to rivet climbing onto next ramp (5.6 R). Climb ramp right for ten feet, then thin nailing past

horizontal cracks and hook moves to a lone bolt, then more nailing and
hooking past a fixed pin, before trending left to a two-bolt belay.
90', 5.6 R A3+

3. From the belay, aid straight up, nailing and hooking expanding flakes,
then up to a right-facing corner and a small roof (fixed pin). Pull over
roof past Bushido death flakes on your left. Climb above roof to a ramp
and belay on the right. 80', 5.8 A4

4. From the belay, climb right ten feet, then up ten feet (wet A2) and left to
a sloping ledge. Trend left to a right-facing corner, climb it past loose
rock above, then follow line of least resistance to the top.

History: Jon Sykes rope-soloed the first two pitches on the 28th and 29th
of June 1997, then finished with the help of Mike Lee on July 6, 1997,
making it back to the cars at 1:15 am, in classic Cannon style.

The Guillotine III 5.10 A2

The Guillotine ascends the center of the steep amphitheater now known
as the Anderson Wall, named in memory of the late Dave Anderson.

1. Start right of center and slab climb to a large ramp.

2. From the left, face climb to white rock below roofs (led on aid, followed
free) to the next large ledge.

3. Make hard boulder move up and left to a ledge, then up steep flakes to
a small belay. 130', 5.10

4. Climb left around a small roof, then back right following small ramp
(aid) to a ledge. Climb up a deep, left-facing chimney and belay on top.

5. Steep, thin cracks lead to an easy ramp and the top.

FA: Dave Anderson and Mike Kenney July 25, 1982

★ Odessa Steps III 5.9 (5.7 R)

Start right of small buttress between Henderson and Muir Buttress.

1. Face climb up and right of black-water streaks to right of buttress. Belay
on ledge twenty feet right of an arching overlap. 150', 5.3

2. Climb on overhanging wall at a weakness (small footholds, but large
buckets). Zigzag up the edge and belay at a platform. 90', 5.6

3. Climb to bushes thirty feet, then traverse left to a large platform. Climb
a left-facing dihedral to the belay 80', 5.6

4. Climb up to the next platform, then jam a hard four-inch crack (crux)
up the dihedral (peg). Belay at its top 110', 5.9

5. Climb loose flakes on left, then back right up a left-facing dihedral to
bushes, traverse right along a ledge to a split block. 80', 5.5

6. Step fifteen feet left, friction up short, overlapping slabs to a ledge, step left once more and face climb to the top. 5.7 R

FA: Howard Peterson and Rob Rittenhouse August, 1972

Touch N'Glow I 5.9

A short crack on the left side of the Muir Buttress.

The name's inspiration was a massage parlor with the same title in Anchorage, Alaska. Start at the base of a shallow crack on the face to the right of a dirty gully.

1. Jam a difficult twenty-foot crack (5.9). Layback to the top of blocks and belay. 80', 5.9

2. Face climb to a delicate mantle shelf (5.8); continue up slabs and blocks to a small tree. Rappel route with two ropes.

FA: Stoney Middleton and Mike Brochu June 3, 1978

Muir III 5.7 R

Start on the left side of the Muir Buttress, the first small buttress to the south (left) of the Whitney-Gilman Ridge.

1. Diagonal up right on easy friction until below a steep wall.

2. Traverse right, then step down to a belay beside a fractured gully. 70', 5.5

3. Climb up the gully's right side; at its top, move right twenty five feet, up ten, then back left twenty five feet to a belay. 80'

4. Step left into yellow gully. Climb poor, unstable rock to its top. Belay on a grass ledge on the right. 90'

5. Traverse right on ledge for 100 feet. Move up past bush to a stance on a slab (peg). 130', 5.4

6. Head left twenty five feet (5.5) to a hard 5.7 crack. 40'

7. Scramble up easy terrain, traversing right to trees.

8. Finish right of Whitney-Gilman Ridge.

FA: Larry Muir, MaryAnn Hooper, and Lee Story May, 1964

Achilles Heel III 5.10

Start on the right side of the Muir Buttress.

1. Climb ramps and headwall up a difficult, short inside corner formed by a large block to an amphitheater capped by a large roof.

2. Break right across the face, then climb up past cracks on a steep headwall to a large ledge on the right.

3. Traverse left across a terrace to a right-facing corner. Climb this to a headwall with horizontal cracks and belay higher. 5.10-

4. Scramble up to a bush-covered ledge that cuts across a large portion of this part of Cannon.

5. Step into a left-facing corner, diagonal left, and climb up to a prominent, left-facing corner leading to the top. 5.9+ (As of this writing, the last pitch of Achilles has detached from the cliff and has become one with the talus slope below. No other information is available.)

FA: Bradley White and Ed Hamilton June, 1984
FFA: Ted Hammond, Andy Jenson, and Bradley White June, 1984
History: Bradley White sliced his achilles tendon on this route, hence the name.

Variation: Too Stoned II 5.10

2a. Climb the first pitch of Achilles Heel, then from the amphitheater, instead of moving right, head left into a right-facing corner, and zig zag via laybacks up to a ledge and rappel from bolts to the ground. 5.10

FA: Bradley White and Jim Shimberg Summer 1987

Ambrosia III 5.8

Begin at the base of a large, hidden, left-facing corner with a hand crack, roughly 100 feet to the left and down from the Whitney-Gilman.

1. The best pitch on this route. Climb the dihedral, by-pass an overhang on the right, and follow the corner crack to a ledge. 100', 5.8

2. Trend left twenty feet to a small tree. Make a delicate, rising traverse farther left, up a little, then back right to a ledge and a tree. 100', 5.7

3. Move left fifteen feet, then make hard moves to a sloping ledge; step right around a corner for twenty-five feet, then ascend a corner on delicate moves to a stance. Layback a block to a belay ledge with bushes. 150'

4. Climb up, then traverse right across an overhanging wall to detached blocks. Make a hard move to a rotten dihedral and junction with the Whitney-Gilman Ridge below the pipe pitch. 80', 5.8

FA: Chris Ellms and Andy Tuthill June, 1975
A shoulder stand was used on pitch three and later free-climbed.

Variation: The Direct Finish II 5.8 A2

4a. Continue straight up, nailing through overhangs to a junction with the Whitney-Gilman Ridge one pitch below the top. 5.8 A2

FA: Andy Tuthill and Chris Rowins Summer, 1978

Eric Pospesil leading the first pitch crack of Ambrosia   Mike Lee

Afternoon sun on Whitney-Gilman

Doug Teschner

★ Meatgrinder   II 5.10+

Below and left of 5.5 direct start to the Whitney-Gilman is the very bottom of the ridge proper. Meatgrinder is twenty feet left and downhill of Chopping Blocking.

1. Jam a strenuous finger crack to bushes and a ledge. 5.10+
2. Climb a left-leaning finger crack (5.10+) twenty feet around a corner onto a slab. Belay on a ledge in a left-facing corner. 5.10+
3. Move up corner (5.9), joining the Whitney-Gilman.

History: Andy Tuthill led the first pitch in May of 1977. Stoney Middleton, Chris Rowins, and Chris Ellms added pitch two and three in 1978.

★ Chopping Blocking   I 5.10a

1. Look for a thin crack that turns to face climbing at the very bottom of the Whitney-Gilman Ridge. 70', 5.10a

FA: Neal Cannon and Jay Dautcher June, 1984

Whitney-Gilman Ridge

★ The Whitney-Gilman   II 5.7

A classic arete climb, as an earlier guidebook author noted, "the uniqueness of a ridge climb makes it an old favorite among locals, and its ascent a ritual."

The preferred start (although not the original one–see variations) is from a ledge on the ridge's east face, which is reached by a scramble up a dirty gully at the bottom of the ridge.

1. Make a couple of face moves up the steep wall, then hand traverse into a prominent right-facing corner (or climb the corner directly via a hand crack 5.6). Follow corner until it is possible to move right onto easier ground. Scramble back left to a huge ledge. 90', 5.5
2. Layback the exposed right edge crack (the left crack is 5.7) to the top of a spike (not obvious from below). Step left onto the face, then up to a second spacious ledge (80', 5.5). Pitch one and two can be combined with 60 meter ropes.
3. Straight up the ridge for 10 feet then out left across a slab and up a slightly awkward V-chimney. Surmount the face, then move back right, avoiding loose blocks, (exposed) to a belay in a corner at the base of a prominent four-inch jam crack. 130', 5.6

4. The classic Pipe Pitch. Up crack and corner (using care not to get your knee stuck in the crack) then out right to an exposed stance at the pipe. High step up left (the route's psychological crux) then face climb to a lower angled face and corner which leads back right across the ridge to a steep, exposed wall. Climb it and belay around the corner to the left. 110', 5.6

5. Up lower-angled rock past a block. Follow obvious foot traverse left to a short inside corner leading to a spacious ledge. Up the obvious inside corner above and razor sharp ridge to airy, standing belay. 110', 5.5

6. Up ridge, trending left following line of least resistance with one awkward move out of a steep alcove (5.7 crux). A final inside corner leads to the top. 110', 5.7

Climber on the exposed Pipe Pitch

Doug Teschner

Variation: Original Start

Start in an obvious gully 70' up the Black Dike talus from the regular start.

1a. Up the easy gully then out right, passing dubious looking blocks. Finish up a corner chimney. (140', 5.4) This brings you to the top of pitch two on the regular route.

★ **The 5.8 Variation**

An exciting alternative in the middle of the route. While it may be hard to believe, the exposure of the pipe move on the regular route is an anticlimax when this variation is followed!

3b. Up the ridge crest heading for an obvious two-inch jam crack. Strenuously climb the crack and the face to its left to a beautiful triangular belay ledge. 80', 5.8

4b. Climb a small inside corner and the blocky, exposed face above, joining the regular route in about fifty feet at the pipe platform.

★ **Variation: The 5.9 Finish**

This used to be the preferred finish at 5.6+ until a block fell off, increasing the difficulty significantly. When climbed with the 5.8 variation, it makes for a more sustained and challenging line.

6a. Ascend directly up the last arete with a tricky start past several pins. Thin crack climbing up the steep headwall leads to the top. 100', 5.9

FA: Unknown

Variation: Right Hand Finish 5.9

6b. Follow the ridge crest over blocks, then up right onto an exposed ledge above the Black Dike. Climb a thin crack up the steep face, followed by an exposed step left to finish. 100', 5.9

History of the Whitney-Gilman Ridge: *Bradley Gilman and Hassler Whitney climbed this classic ridge without the use of pitons on August 3, 1929, accomplishing what was at the time, the hardest climb in America. The route was originally climbed in 17 short pitches, and is now climbed in as little as three 60-meter pitches.*

Across the Great Divide III 5.7 A4 (or 5.11)

This is an exposed aid climb up the dark north wall of the Whitney-Gilman Ridge. Bring a standard A4 rack on this seldom-climbed beauty. Look for a shallow dihedral that is the start of the climb and now goes free at 5.11 or 5.7, A3.

1. Climb up the dihedral, then out right across a smooth wall to a two-bolt belay around the corner. 130', 5.7 A3 (or 5.11)
2. Climb diagonally right to access a crack that shoots up almost the entire wall. Two bolt belay. 140', 5.6 A3
3. When the crack ends, nail straight up the wall, thin aid. 75', A4
4. Drop down left, then nail a short dihedral which joins the Whitney-Gilman Ridge to the top.

History: Peter Cole and Rick Wilcox climbed the first pitch; Cole, Mark Richey, and Rainsford Rouner led pitch two; Cole and Wilcox completed the ascent in November, 1975. Jim Surette and Steve Larson freed pitch one in the spring of 1985.

Variation: The Direct Finish IV 5.8 A4

A more sustained finish to an already difficult aid climb.

3a. Ascend twenty feet of regular A4 pitch, then trend up and right following shallow corner systems to a small ledge. 150', A4
4a. Climb up and right through steep corners, traversing below a large, barely attached block to the top. 140', 5.8 A3

FA: Chris Rowins and Brad White August, 1985

The Black Dike

Grade unknown. Not recommended.

History: The third route to be climbed on Cannon, done by Arthur Emmons and Will Jenks on October 13, 1930.

Rockfall occurs daily in the dike and should only be climbed during winter. Even then, rockfall is a problem.

The D'Arcy Route

Grade unknown. Not recommended.

This route ascends the steep wall above Cannonade Buttress. Loose rock makes this route and others in this area very dangerous, and in the author's opinion, not worth the risk.

FA: Ray D'Arcy and Bill Crouther 1958

Cannonade II 5.4

This is the easiest route on Cannon, yet loose rock and route finding make this a serious undertaking. At 5.5, Lakeview is by far the best beginner route.

1. Climb the south (left) side of the buttress to the top. Belay either from

a tree or a two-bolt anchor. 140′, 5.2

2. Make a long traverse to the right moving across the face with very little protection to a belay before a corner. Look for fixed pegs. 120′, 5.2

3. Climb corner, move around nose and up a ramp on right, then step left over blocks to a slab and twin, inside corners.

4. Ascend the right-hand dihedral to the trees. Finish up left.

FA: Leigh Andrews and Earle Whipple May 3, 1964

Parawing III 5.10

Begin two feet left of English Cowboy.

1. Climb finger crack in white granite that closes twenty-five feet up (5.10), then up a corner and easy crack to a belay. 130′, 5.10

2. Follow same line, slightly left of a corner with loose blocks. 140′, 5.7

3. Easy slabs lead up to a steep bulge. Take the crack/small corner up and right, then back left into the main line to the top of the crack. Step down to a finger crack, go left, then back right on easier blocks and cracks to the original line. 140′, 5.9

4. Unprotected slab-climbing leads up and slightly right to a rectangular block. Belay at small tree. 155′, 5.8

5 - 7. Finish up slabs, bad rock, bushes, etc or rappel.

History: Chris Rowins and Andy Tuthill did the majority of the route in August of 1976. George Hurley and Kurt Winkler added a possibly more direct finish described above, on June 7, 1985.

English Cowboy I 5.8

Located on the right side of Cannonade Buttress are two right-facing dihedrals.

1. Climb the left dihedral to its top. 120′, 5.8

FA: Chris Ellms and John Powell June, 1977

★ The British Were Coming IV 5.8

This is a serious route at 5.8 that has seen much rockfall over the past few years. In my opinion this is alpine 5.8 for 5.10 leaders with full mental commitment. Start in the right dihedral just north of English Cowboy.

1. Climb the dark corner, then into the V-groove on the left wall until on top of the buttress. 120′, 5.8

2. Traverse right to a small, left-facing corner, then up and left, zigzagging up a fractured white slab to a ledge. 150′, 5.8

3. Climb diagonally right to a large, left-facing corner, up the corner and follow crack to a belay. 150′, 5.6

4. Traverse left across a sloping slab to a weakness. Climb it to a belay at the base of a large, left-facing bomb-bay chimney. 70′

5. Enter the chimney, and start jamming to its top, then undercling out left with little protection to a stance in an alcove. 120′, 5.8

6. Head left, climb the slab above, keeping right of a large dihedral, and belay on a ledge with a birch tree. 150′, 5.6

7. Move right ten feet, then head straight through overlaps to a belay on top of a horizontally split block. 150′, 5.7

8. You can scratch out one more pitch, top-out, and hike off.

FA: Andy Tuthill and Chris Ellms August 9, 1975. They beat Doug Madara and Paul Ross (of the UK) by several days, hence the name.

Fugue IV 5.10

"A long, adventurous free climb, with virtuoso climbing on nearly every pitch," wrote Ed Webster in Rock Climbs in the White Mountains of New Hampshire. When the book was written in 1986 this was a great route. Now, after fourteen years, and many rockslides, this is a deadly climb that is better left alone. Start left of Quartet below a right diagonal V-corner twenty feet up.

1. Climb up twenty feet, step right on a foot ledge, and ascend the V-dihedral to a narrow belay. 130′, 5.9

2. Step left twenty feet to a small, right-facing corner, up the corner twenty feet (5.10) to an overlap and a left-facing corner. At its top, move left twelve feet under an overlap to a small ledge. 120′, 5.10

3. At the ledge's right end, climb above the overlap, angle back left to a finger crack, climb the crack and move left to an easier crack heading to a higher overlap and a semi-hanging belay. 130′, 5.9

4. Trend right over the overlap at a horn, then move past another overlap above to easy steps and a twelve-foot high, left-facing corner rising above a traverse ledge cutting across the entire face. (One can escape left to Cannonade.) Layback the corner, climb up and left to a difficult face (one 5.10 move) heading farther left. Follow face holds up right to another ledge. 140′, 5.10

5. Climb a finger crack and corner above to a twelve foot traverse, left to another crack/corner. Climb this to a ledge, step left a few feet following an easy left-slanting corner to the top of a pointed slab with a fixed piton (junction with Hanson-Echardt). 130′, 5.9

6. Climb twenty-five feet right, then up, heading for an inside corner in the major overlap high above. Continue past a ledge (and large broken blocks), angle up left, then up and right to the inside corner and the key to the final overlap. 150′, 5.8

7. Climb the overlap by the corner (the original line, 5.10 R) or move about twelve feet right to a broken dihedral (5.8 variation). Climb this for twenty feet, then back left to re-join the original corner. 145′, 5.10 R or 5.8

FA: George Hurley and Ian Turnbull August 17, 1983

Marc Chauvin, Paul Ross, and Hurley were involved with the first four pitches and finished left in three more pitches on June 17, 1983. John Bouchard and George Hurley made the second ascent of the direct route in September of 1983 avoiding the final 5.10 R section with the 5.8 variation on the right. They climbed it in seven pitches as described above.

Quartet

Grade unknown, not recommended.

Quartet ascends the rotten gully in the back of the corner on the left side of Duet Buttress, then follows faint vertical dike system to the left of Duet.
FA: Frank Carey, Ray D'Arcy, Harry King, and Gordon Weston 1956

★ Duet Arete I 5.9+

Ascends the arete between Quartet and Hanson-Echardt.

1. Fifteen feet right of Quartet, climb a corner, step up and right onto edges. Belay under a roof. 135′, 5.8

2. Surmount an overhang (5.9), step right (pitons). Climb a shallow right-facing corner (5.9+) laybacking to small, bush-covered ledges. Jam a crack, then traverse right to top of Hanson-Echardt's second pitch. 5.9+ Rappel with two ropes.

FA: John Mallery and Jim Fitzpatrick September, 1980

The Hanson-Echardt Memorial IV 5.10

Just left of Duet Buttress are two parallel, vertical corners; Hanson-Echardt is the left corner; Duet is in the right corner. This route, Fugue, and The British Were Coming, all have had recent rock-fall and are considered very dangerous. The second pitch is highly recommended and is accessible via the Duet first pitch.

1. Ascend a corner to a small ledge, then move right around the corner to a ledge above. 100′, 5.8

2. Follow a flake to the base of the dihedral. Chimney and stem the corner (5.10) to the top of the buttress. 130′, 5.10

3. Easy climbing to the Duet Garden.

4. Ascend a short wall to the base of the upper slabs.

5. Traverse left for some distance on a narrow ledge to the third, right-facing, inside corner. Climb the corner (5.9) to a belay stance. 5.9

6. Hard (5.9) climbing to the corner's top. Ascend cracks on the left to a small corner. Belay at blocks. 5.9

7. Trend left along a flake, then down and thirty feet left to a break. Belay on a sloping ledge. 5.7

8. Climb over one overlap, then a second (5.8), and exit left to the trees.

History: Ed Webster and Bryan Delaney completed the first ascent of the route on May 18, 1974, in memory of two friends, Bob Hanson and Caroline Echardt. They were killed by rockfall at Quincy Quarries near Boston in December, 1973. Sam Streibert and Al Rubin freed the entire route in May of 1977.

Shad Lawton leading the classic second pitch of Duet

Jamie Cunningham

★ Duet III 5.7

The pitches above the Duet Garden are loose and detract from the enjoyable climbing below. Most parties rappel after the first two or three pitches.

1. Ascend the crack and corner to a small ledge. Layback and jam up the crack to a belay above the short chimney. 120′, 5.7

2. Move up and right a few feet, then enter the crack and diagonally climb right across the upper part of Duet Buttress. 125′, 5.6

3. Climb up easy ground to the Duet Garden.

4. Follow a rotten gully and slabs to a second, higher garden.

5. Follow grassy dike above the left end of the garden to a large, sloping ledge on the right. Belay on the right end. 80′

6. Make a long step to a loose spike, then move up and left until beneath a triangular overhang. Avoid this by climbing slabs to the right to finish.

FA: Phil Nelson and Alan Wedgewood (UK) May 23, 1964

★ Variation: Duet Direct I 5.10

1. Climb Duet's first pitch. 5.7

2a. An incredible pitch. Jam and layback the sustained, left-facing dihedral to the top of the Duet Buttress. 5.10

FA: Michael Hartrich and Tom Schwarm July, 1974

Extinct belay on Duet Direct

Mike Lee

★ The Wrong Crack II 5.11 [or 5.10 A0]

On the left side of Duet Buttress at the lowest point is a small, right-facing corner.

1. Layback up the corner to some loose, stacked flakes. Climb up into a chimney to a tiny belay ledge.
2. Move up the chimney, laybacking up a dihedral (5.11), or climb right and down to a small bush, then ascend a left-arching crack to a hard move back to the corner. Layback the corner for ten feet, then move left around the corner into the face and up to a hanging belay at a horizontal crack. 90', 5.10
3. Ascend diagonally right to a small stance in a corner. Move right (5.11) or tension (A0) into a thin crack. Head to a 5.6 chimney and a ledge on the left. 5.11 or 5.9 A0
4. Climb Raven Crack's second pitch to the top of the buttress or rappel off.

History: The first pitch was climbed by Roger Martin and Chuck Zaikowski in 1973 and called Chimney Sweep. In the spring of 1976, Chris Ellms and Andy Tuthill climbed the second pitch and connected with Duet by an incredible finger traverse. The entire route was finally climbed by Chris Ellms and Roger Martin in 1977. The direct start to pitch two was done by Andy Tuthill and Chester Dreiman in the fall of 1981, and the tension traverse on pitch three was free climbed by Neil Cannon with Jay Dautcher in July, 1984.

★ The Right Stuff II 5.11

1. Climb the Sextet finger crack, step right into the Wrong Crack chimney (pitch one). 120', 5.8
2. Directly above the belay, climb up a corner (5.11). (Wrong Crack traverses right fifteen feet.) Ascend left up the crack onto the face to the same belay as Wrong Crack. 60', 5.11
3. Climb the crack left into a corner, then make a hard traverse right (5.11) into a thin crack that leads to the 5.6 chimney. 130', 5.11

FFA: Neil Cannon with Jay Dautcher July, 1984

★ Sextet III 5.11 A0

Sextet begins in the thin, vertical finger crack between Duet and Wrong Crack.

1. Ascend the thin finger crack past two fixed pitons, then stem up and right (5.11) to another thinner crack. Step right into a hard layback (5.10+) and climb up the chimney to a small stance. 130', 5.11

Eric Pospesil taking it Slow & Easy

Jon Sykes

2. Step right from the corner, then climb a thin finger crack up the center of the slab. At the top of the crack, step right and belay. 5.11 A0

3. Climb a crack up a white face high up on the Duet Buttress to a belay on the right. 5.8

4. Head right around a slab to a corner. Continue up and right to a break in the slab and belay. 5.7

5. Climb up and right again, to join with Icarus. Ascend the slab right of the broken open book and belay on top of it.

6. Climb the crack up the corner to a notch, through this, then out the right side of a second notch to a slab that joins the fifth pitch of Sam's Swan Song above the Cow Pasture.

History: Bradley White and Andy Crane led pitch one with a little aid in August, 1985. Dave Karl, Ted Hammond, and Bradley White freed pitch one later that month. Bradley White and Andy Byerly made the complete ascent of the route in July, 1986.

★ Slow and Easy I 5.8

This is a beautiful, yet tricky, arching crack.
1. Climb the right arching crack left of Sticky Fingers.
FA: Roger Martin and Chuck Zaikowski 1973

★ Sticky Fingers I 5.10

The stunning, right-leaning finger crack on the right side of a clean face, 50 feet north of the Duet Buttress. (Notice rockfall scar on face and crater on ground between Slow and Easy and Sticky fingers—summer 1999.)

1. Jam and friction up the finger crack to a belay in a right-facing corner. 60', 5.10

2. Face climb up and left (bolt), then up the face past two more bolts with difficulty to a two-bolt anchor on top of a buttress. 50', 5.10

History: Bryan Delaney and Howard Peterson cleaned and climbed the first pitch in August, 1974. A month later Peterson rappel bolted the second pitch, then led it.

★ Raven Crack II 5.9

Above Slow and Easy is a right-facing dihedral with an incredible vertical crack system. This climb has been upgraded from 5.8 to 5.9.

1. Scramble third class on the left to the top of Sticky Fingers Buttress, or climb Slow and Easy to a two-bolt belay. 90'

2. Jam and layback the beautiful crack system (5.9) to a small belay with pins. 60', 5.9

The author at the top of the second pitch of Midlife Crisis   Steve Dupuis

3. Step left (tricky) into more crack climbing and a stance. Move left then up cracks and third class to the top right side of Duet Buttress. 140', 5.8 Most parties scramble up and over left to a belay on Duet Direct for rappelling to the ground.

FA: John Drew and Paul (Base) Boissonneault March, 1976
FFA: Andy Tuthill and Chris Ellms May, 1977

★ Rodan II 5.11b

Formerly known as Icarus, this route now goes free. The A4 section on pitch three was not to be found on the free ascent probably due to the winter conditions on the first ascent. The route starts in the corner just right of the Sticky Fingers Buttress and follows a corner system right of Raven Crack. This was the first route to be pioneered on Cannon in winter.

1. Climb the easy corner just right of Sticky Fingers to a two-bolt belay.
2. From the belay, climb the face up to the overhang (bolt) and up into the corner following it to a bolt belay. 5.11b
3. Climb the corner for about 80 feet, then traverse left onto the front of the Duet Buttress and belay a little higher up on a ledge. 150'
4. through **7**. Above the Duet Buttress there are many ways to continue:

All of them are loose and constantly moving. It is my opinion that the route, as described in 1974, has changed so dramatically for the worse, that it is no longer advisable to provide a route description. All route descriptions in this area are vague at best. It is best to follow your instincts while climbing above the Duet Buttress.

FA: John Bouchard and Rick Wilcox January, 1974
FFA: Jim Shimberg and Bradley White September, 1989

★ Midlife Crisis IV 5.9 A4

After completing the second ascent four years after the historic first ascent, I have nothing but praise for this bold, technical aid climb. It is located in the center of the sweeping wall between Duet Buttress on the left, and the Triple S Buttress to the right. Appropriately named, Paul's Wall is an impressive series of labyrinths and steep slabs. Midlife Crisis cuts the middle of this with climbing similar to, but harder than, The Ghost. A complete aid rack is needed.

1. Start on top of two huge stacked blocks 40' left of the start of Sam's Swan Song. Climb up, then right of ledges to a two-piton belay on top of a block. 130', 5.8

2. Mixed climbing leads up, then left to a pin up two right-facing, inside corners. Climb these to a headwall. A piton and a rivet bypass a tempting placement behind a suspicious block on the left. Surmount the headwall to a bolt and free climb a slab to a three-piton belay below a roof. 130', 5.7 A4

3. Move out right from belay to a bolt, then up and out the right-hand side of the roof. Gently nail an expanding flake to a small ledge. Climb left toward loosely stacked blocks. A rivet bypasses these blocks and eventually leads to the security of a bolt. Holes and rivets lead to the belay. 140', A3

4. Climb the ramp up and left past deeply drilled rivets (hanger-less bolts) to a bolt. Climb the thin flake to the terrace. Move hard right, climbing across the top of huge blocks, then up to a two-bolt belay at a grass ledge. 90', 5.8

5. Move right eight to ten feet and climb up a groove past pitons and bolts to the Cow Pasture belay on Sam's Swan Song (80', 5.9). Finish up Sam's or rappel the route.

FA: Paul Cormier, Jon Eagleson, Greg Cloutier, and Trevor Hamilton.
History: The route was done in September, 1994, in three pushes.

★ Sam's Swan Song III 5.7

Despite its reputation for accidents and epics, this is perhaps New Hampshire's best "mountaineering" rock route, due to its length, complex route-finding, loose rock, and yes, even some good climbing! It's a serious undertaking with a real feeling of commitment. There is no easy escape and rappelling off is problematic due to the length, loose rock, and (in places) the zig-zagging nature of the route. Wait for good weather , get an early start, avoid climbing below other parties, and have a great adventure.

WARNING: Pitch three was cleaned of tons of rock by Mark Richey in 1998 while seconding the pitch. He sustained a fractured arm and rappelled to the ground with John Bouchard and walked out.

Start at the prominent large left-facing corner on the left side of Sam's Buttress (the first buttress to the left of the Big Wall section and well to the right of the Duet Buttress). Lightning Crack is a more enjoyable start to Sam's Swan Song.

1. Up cracks, flakes, and the corner to a ledge with bolts where the climbing eases, 20' below the top of the buttress. 120', 5.7
2. Move left on an easy-rising traverse ledge to a stance below, and to the left of a rotten, orange-ish dike. 90', 5.2 (Pitch 2 and 3 can be combined with double 60 meter ropes.)
3. A thin move right gains the loose and poorly protected dike/corner system which is followed to a ledge at the base of a left-facing layback corner. 95', 5.5
4. Up corner (or loose dike) to top of blocks. Move right (onto a wall hidden from below) following a classic rising traverse to a small stance atop a short, left-facing corner. 90', 5.6
5. Climb straight up (many variations) to the Cow Pasture. 120', 5.4
6. Careful route-finding needed: climb a right-slanting crack then head for a prominent 10' high off-width crack (actually 2 parallel cracks but only one is visible from below). At the top of the cracks, move 20' up and right on cleaned rock to a 10-foot high, steep, south-facing wall which is climbed to an exposed ledge. (Note: Many parties have gotten lost here by heading left rather than climbing the final steep wall.) 90', 5.7-
7. Make an awkward step right "across the void" (or, harder, climb straight up and right from the belay), then follow the cracks and a left-facing corner to a large, down-sloping ledge. 60', 5.7
8. Start at the left end of the ledge and climb up over blocks for 8', then 30' left along a large horizontal crack. Continue traversing left for 30' more

Gareth Slattery following the traverse on pitch two of Sam's Swan Song

Jon Sykes

(passing a harder dihedral), then back right up a blocky corner/gully. Trend rightward up the slab above to a grassy ledge with a bolt. 130', 5.5

9. Move up a short friction slab and the grassy, mossy, bushy corner above for 80'. Move left at an obvious break and pull up through a notch in an overhanging bulge. Continue to a grassy ledge. 140', 5.6

10 & 11. 250' of third class climbing up and right leads to the trail along the top of the cliff.

History: The first attempt was in July, 1964, by John Reppy and Jim McCarthy. They climbed the initial buttress but McCarthy was drawn (understandably) to the VMC arch which they attempted that day. A little later Alan Wedgewood (UK), Sam Streibert, and Phil Nelson made it to the Cow Pasture before they turned back. The historic first complete ascent was made by Alan Wedgewood, Phil Nelson, and Mike and Sally Westmacott (UK) in August of 1964.

Variation #1: Native Son I 5.9

1a. Climb the chimney twenty feet left of Sam's first pitch, then up the left-facing dihedral to the top of the first pitch of Sam's. 150', 5.9

FA: John Porter and friend, 1964

★ Variation #2: Lightning Crack I 5.7

1b. Climb thirty feet up Sam's corner, then step left into Lightning Crack and jam and layback up the crack to its end and a belay on the right. 150', 5.7

FA: Unknown

Variation #3: Sam's Ghost II 5.10

1. Gain the top of Triple S Buttress.

2. Head up the left side of a brown dike. Climb small corners and flakes, pull over a bulge to a crack. Ascend the cracks to a corner, climb up this to a wide crack and belay. 150', 5.9

3. Up more cracks and a steep dike of loose rock to small roofs. Climb the roofs up and right to a ledge, then up the face to the third belay on Sam's Swan Song. 120', 5.10

FA: Ted Hammond and Bradley White June 8, 1983

FFA: Same June 9, 1983

★ Variation #4: Fall From Grace I 5.12b

Climb the first twenty feet of Sinister Satisfaction, then step left (pin) and follow a line of bolts to the belay on top of Triple S buttress.

FA: Chris Gill late 1980s

★ Variation #5: Sinister Satisfaction I 5.8

Look on the right side of Triple S, and you'll see twin dihedrals.

1. Ascend the left-hand corner. A tricky start with great climbing above. 150', 5.8

FA: Howard Peterson and Joe Bridges July, 1974

Gareth Slattery leading the testy Sinister Satisfaction

Jamie Cunningham

★ Hierophont Tower II 5.11a

From the top of Triple S Buttress look for the distinct right-facing corner just left of the top of the buttress leading to a steep, bolt-protected face.

1. Climb Lightning Crack to its top and belay at the bolt anchor just below the top of Triple S to your right. 5.7

2. From the belay head left and climb through a break in a roof. Move up a shallow dike (bolt), then left on small ledges and flakes. Mantle up to a shallow corner and climb the corner, then hard traverse right to a large crack. Up the crack to a belay and rappel the route, or do one more pitch to the Ghost roof (pitch described below).

3. From the ledge move up and right to an A1 move past a bolt to handholds, and run it out to the Ghost Roof.

History: The first ascent is unknown. An old bolt and pin were found lower down on the route. Jim Shimberg freed a variation corner left after the dike on the second pitch at 5.10. Bradley White, Jim Shimberg, and Jody Crawford were all part of the first (documented) ascent in the summer of 1989.

The Big Wall

Located in the center of Cannon Cliff, The Big Wall section is home of five grade five routes. (Some of the most difficult and longest routes on the East Coast.) The Big Wall stands between Triple S Buttress on the left and the Conn Buttress to the right.

★ The Ghost IV 5.7 A3

Just right of Triple S buttress is a white streak four hundred feet up on a steep slab, The Ghost. This is a great route for training, and if you want a Grade V, connect it with the Ghost Roof (IV 5.9 A4.) Combining these two makes for a commanding two-day adventure, or a speedy one-day ascent. The entire climb can be done with clean aid.

1. & 2. Climb the right side corner of the Triple S Buttress, (one pitch with a 60-meter rope) and belay at the base of a right diagonal crack.

3. Clean aid the crack to a bolt and dowel ladder, up this to a sloping belay in the middle of The Ghost. 110', A2 (Pitch three and four can be combined by using a 60-meter rope.)

4. Climb the A1 bolt ladder to a hanging belay under the roof. 60', A1

5. Climb the Perverse Traverse left under the large overlap, step down, then left and up a corner (bolt). Aid up and right to a horizontal flake and belay on top. 80', A3

6. Climb mixed ground up a groove and corner to a ledge beneath blocky roofs (The Ghost Roof). Two-bolt belay. 100', 5.7 A3

7. to 9. Traverse left and up Sam's Swan Song (5.7) or climb The Ghost Roof (A4) for a real Grade V big wall.

FA: Paul Ross, John Bragg, and Michael Peloquin July, 1971

The Ghost Roof IV 5.9 A4

The direct line through the ominous roof system above pitch 6 of The Ghost. In the opinion of the author, combining The Ghost and The Ghost Roof naturally creates No. 6 for Grade V big wall climbs on Cannon.

6a. From the horizontal flake, ascend a groove 40 feet. Move right to a small ledge at a horizontal crack. 5.8, A2

7a. Climb up to an obvious break in the overhangs. Aid up a right-facing wall, move horizontally right ten feet, up and back left through the roofs (A4) to a steep slab. Climb mixed ground left to a ledge. A4

8a. and 9a. Climb two more full pitches of 5.5 to 5.6 to the top.

FA: Chris Ellms, Andy Tuthill, and Stoney Middleton June, 1978. The entire route saw its first and second clean ascents in the summer of 1997 by Jim Shimberg and Jim Westgate, followed a week later by Jon Sykes and Steve Dupuis.

★ One Drop of Water V 5.9 A3 (or 5.11 X AO)

This is a commanding route that seldom gets climbed. A very direct line up the left center of the Big Wall. All free except for one point of aid.

1. Just right of the start of VMC Direct is a vertical dike. Free climb up the dike for eighty feet, then left into a corner, then right into another short corner. From here, climb to a large, leaning fin and belay on top of the fin. One bolt, 180'

2. From the belay, climb the arch and dike up to a belay on VMC Direct. 160'

3. Climb VMC Direct until under the huge overlap. Head left under overlap thirty or so feet; two old bolts over the lip of the overhang will lead you to a two-bolt belay on top of horizontal crack (rope drag). 160'

4. From the belay, step right and mantle up to an expanding flake. Climb this (be careful) to a weakness in a short vertical wall, and belay above at fixed pins on a slab. FA Bivy. 150', 5.9 A2

5. Move left by-passing the slab, then aid back right twenty feet. Climb on difficult aid through blocky roofs and belay at twin finger cracks. 100', A3 (or 5.11 X AO)

6. Jam the striking finger cracks up the exposed slab above the roof system. 165'

7. & 8. Easy 5.3 to 5.6 climbing up blocky slabs leads to the top.

History: Jeff Pheasant and Paul Ross completed the first ascent on July 16 and 17, 1976. They spent an epic night in their bivouac pinned down by a torrential downpour. They named their route after a quote by Emilio

Comici, "Let one drop of water fall from the summit, and that is the line I shall follow."

Neal Cannon with Alison Osius free climbed all but one point of aid, on pitch 5, in the summer of 1984.

★ VMC Direct V 5.11

The first Grade V big wall aid climb on the East Coast, completed in 1965, and the first Grade V free climb in the East, led in 1974. If you intend to aid climb this route, please use existing fixed pins and natural gear to protect the quality of the rock. A hammer should be used only to test the integrity of existing fixed gear. Look for the largest left-hand arch on the left side of The Big Wall.

1. Climb up the right side corner of Triple S Buttress to a belay at the start of the right-leaning arch. 5.5
2. Ascend the arch, trend out right a few moves rejoining the arch again. Then move across the face to a belay stance. 5.10
3. Layback and undercling to where the two arches meet. Pull through the overlap and face climb the dike to the huge overlap. Bolt belay. 5.9+
4. Climb up to a roof, undercling right, then face climb across a very hard traverse. Belay at a small stance above on the right. Bolt belay. 5.11
5. Make hard friction moves above the belay (5.11), or out right and up (5.10 R). Proceed past a flake traversing left to a shallow dihedral, followed by easy slabs. Climb a small overlap to a headwall, bolt belay. 5.11 or 5.10 R
6. Climb over the headwall, moving right, then up a shallow left-facing corner to slabs. Move past a large spike on the left, and up unprotected loose rock to a belay on the left side of the Cow's Mouth. 5.10
7. Make hard undercling moves out the right side roof crack (many fixed pins) of the Cow's Mouth, to easy climbing. 5.10+
8. & 9. Head up the line of least resistance following slabs and cracks trending right and to the top. 5.5/5.6

History: In July, 1964, Jim McCarthy belayed by John Reppy made the first attempt on the route getting part way up the first arch. Later that year, Dick Williams attempted the route several times with different partners including Jim McCarthy, John Reppy, Ants Leemets, Dave Craft, and Art Gran. On one attempt in October of 1964, Dick Williams, Art Gran, and John Reppy climbed the first three pitches, retreating after a snowstorm. Finally in September, 1965, after partying all night, and a bivouac for added adventure, Dick Williams, Yvon Chouinard, and Art Gran made the historic first ascent. The equally impressive first free ascent was climbed in

July, 1974, by Bob Anderson and Sam Streibert, leading the way for future free ascents of the bigger routes.

Variation start: The Mini-Direct I 5.10

1a. Ascend the right-side corner of Triple S Buttress to a small, right-facing corner with a crack below the VMC Direct arch. 80', 5.4

2a. Climb to the corner, and layback with difficulty up thirty feet connecting with VMC Direct's second pitch. 5.10

FA: Unknown

FFA: Andy Tuthill and Josh Lieberman July 4, 1982

★ VMC Direct Direct IV 5.10+

A Cannon classic, the Direct Direct's dihedrals are some of the finest in the East. This is a sought after climb both free and on clean aid only. Ascend the right corner on a smaller white buttress just north of Triple S Buttress.

1. Climb the corner to the top of the buttress. 100', 5.7

2. Work your way up a short, right-leaning dihedral, then left on a ramp,

Tim Kemple, Sr., starting the third pitch variation of VMC Direct Direct
Tim Kemple, Jr.

then back right, underclinging an overlap to a right-facing corner, up this to a bolt belay. 120', 5.10+

3. Make hard moves off the belay into the next corner, up this to an overhang. The original aid line pulls the roof and climbs a blind corner on the left (5.10+, small wires, pins, and bolts). Or continue up the corner underclinging and laybacking past Base's Flake, then left to a corner, up this to the same belay. Two bolts. 130', 5.10

4. Climb rotten rock to a bolt, then move left to a right-facing corner, move left onto the face and a lone bolt. Face climb to a corner, up this left to a two-bolt belay above. 120', 5.9

5.-9. Finish up VMC Direct.

History: Steve Arsenault and Sam Streibert completed the first ascent in wet conditions on June 7-8, 1969, while Arsenault was on leave from Vietnam. In June, 1975, Jeff Burns freed the route with Hans Larsen. Paul (Base) Boissonneault, Gene Vallee, and Chris Rowins freed Base's Flake (the third pitch variation) in August, 1978.

★ Variation: Raging Rainbow II A4

1. Climb first pitch of VMC Direct Direct. 5.7

2a. Follow second pitch up to an arch, and look for the seam over the arch three feet from its end. Nail the seam straight up, thinner near the top. Bat hook over a small overlap to a two-bolt belay. 160', A3+

3a. From the belay, nail up to and through a headwall to a right diagonal seam. Hard micro-nailing up the seam to its end, then step right into the right-facing corner of Direct Direct's third pitch, and to the belay. 80', A4

History: While nailing the crux of pitch three, Jon Sykes and Eric Carpenter were caught in an unexpected thunderstorm which forced Jon to finish the pitch in a raging waterfall. Forty minutes later the rain stopped, the sun came out, and a double rainbow appeared in the Notch.

FA: Jon Sykes and Eric Carpenter August 23, 1999

★ Variation: More Direct I 5.9+/5.10a

1a. This fun outing climbs the first one hundred feet of Stryder Wall and then ascends the right-facing corner just right of VMC Direct Direct's second pitch. 180'

FA: Eric Carpenter and Jon Sykes October 23, 2000

Eric Carpenter cleans the first ascent of Raging Rainbow

Jon Sykes

★ Stryder Wall   IV 5.8 A3

Ascends the steep blank wall between VMC Direct Direct and Labyrinth Wall. A sustained route when connected with Labyrinth Wall Direct. Start at a short, narrow corner to the right of Direct Direct.

1. Climb the corner and face climb past a 1/4″ bolt to another small corner. Belay on a small ledge left of Labyrinth Wall. 5.7

2. Climb left, then past dowels to a large, sloping ledge. Aid on scary bolts to a steep, arching crack. Up this to a hanging belay. 5.7 A2

3. Ascend the bolt ladder up the steep blank wall to a small ledge, continue up more bolts to a hanging belay below a roof. A1

4. Climb up right following a crack to a mantle shelf, then face climb with little protection to a small ledge. 5.7 A1

5. Ascend a thin line for twenty feet joining Labyrinth Wall at the "A4 (now free at 5.11) seam" below a ledge.

6.-10. Follow Labyrinth Wall Direct to the top to create a commanding Grade V Big Wall.

FA: Steve Schneider and Doug McBride Summer, 1978

★ Labyrinth Wall Direct V 5.11 (5.10 R) or 5.8 A2

This is one of the longest sustained Big Wall free climbs in the East. If you choose to aid climb the route, please do it as cleanly as possible. The climb starts fifty feet right of VMC Direct Direct. Third class up seventy feet below the left side of a large, horizontal overlap.

1. Climb past a bolt and pins in a shallow corner, then up face to overlap. Head left, then up left side of overlap to a two-bolt belay. 130', 5.10

2. Head right and climb a left-facing corner, then right again and up to a

The author wakes up on Stryder Wall   Steve Dupuis

belay. 5.8

3. Free climb past three bolts on steep face. Then angle left and climb to the higher of two ledges in the Amphitheater. 5.10+

4. Hard moves past bolts lead out the left side of the amphitheater to a bolt belay. 5.11

5. To free this pitch head out right from belay face climbing (bolts) to an overlap, then climb a steep wall on the right to a small fixed belay. To aid the pitch, follow dowels above belay to overlap, then aid right to the steep wall, up this to same belay. 5.11 (or A2)

6. Friction left to bolts, step left under an overlap, then step over it to the right of a thin, vertical crack (5.8 R), up right to a small stance.

6a. Climb the vertical "A4 seam" on the left, the original aid line, which now climbs free at 5.11 or A2.

7. Climb back left under a short arch to a bivi ledge. 35', 5.11

The A4 seam and the 5.11 free pitch end up at the same bivi ledge. 5.11

Labyrinth Wall Direct Finish 5.11 (5.10+ R)

8. Traverse 30' left along a horizontal flake, climb over a break (crux) then head up to a stance, with three good, half-driven knife blades for a belay. 5.10+ (5.8 R)

9. Climb right on slab below a huge arch. Five bolt belay. 60', 5.11 (5.10+ R)

10. Angle left staying generally below and left of the aid route's fixed gear. Climb up a thin flake to a steep open corner right of a large slab. Climb open corner to a large, bushy ledge. 5.10+ (5.10 R)

12.-14. Climb the short, steep corner above two slabs, then easy scrambling to the top. 5.6

★ Walk on the Wild Side IV 5.11

8a. Above the bivi ledge, climb up a right-facing corner that arches to the right. Follow a flake right (5.10), then face climb up to a belay ledge with a two-bolt belay. 5.10

9a. Same as YMC Dike, face climb up a dike (5.8+), or exit right (with a short rappel off a tree) to an easy gully and the top.

History: Paul Ross and Michael Pelaquin climbed the first ascent of the first seven pitches on August 12-13, 1971, finishing up YMC Dike to the top. Peter Cole, Rainsford Rouner and Mark Hudon completed Labyrinth Wall Direct using the direct finish in November, 1974, after several unsuccessful attempts. Chris Kulezycki and partner free climbed the first five pitches in 1979. Bob Rotert and Mark Richey made the first free ascent to the top using the Walk on the Wild Side finish in seven hours on May 24,

1981. Labyrinth Wall Direct finally saw its first free ascent—but not without a fight: Neal Cannon and Tor Raubenheimer were zapped off the cliff two pitches up by lightening on the first attempt. Cannon and Jay Dautcher were stopped by wet rock on the second attempt. Finally in October, 1984, Neal Cannon and Alison Osius freed the entire route in six hours. The original A4 seam was free climbed by Jim Shimberg after placing two bolts in the early 1990s.

Variation: Lost in the Ozone 5.10+

6a. Climb up and right to a horizontal crack (pin), move up to a large roof, then right past a shaky piton (5.10+), and climb over the roof. Continue straight to a horizontal crack and a nut belay. 5.10+

7a. Follow a slab under a large overlap, which slants to the right to join the upper part of YMC Dike. 5.8

History: Gerry Handron and Steve Larson made the first ascent while lost on Lab Wall. They may have free climbed part of the upper section of Benedictus Direct.

★ Lowther Memorial (a.k.a. Meltdown) IV 5.12b (5.9 R)

This is the most recent route on the Big Wall. The climbing, although hard, has some of the cleanest rock on Cannon. Locate a mini-buttress 75' right of the start of Labyrinth Wall. The route starts in the middle of the face of the buttress. Look for two pins in the right diagonal crack.

1. Climb the thin slab to crack and first pin, past one more pin and a ledge. Up the next face past a dubious, fixed rurp and pin, then follow crack to top of buttress and a two-bolt belay. 80', 5.9R (You can fourth class up the left side of the buttress.)

2. From belay head left, then up face (hidden pro) and through overlap to three bolts on a steep face. Face climb with increasing difficulty past the three bolts (5.11d), then step down and right and mantle (5.10d) to a shallow, left-facing corner (pin). Ascend the corner, arching left to a large labyrinth in the center of the lower part of the Big Wall. Over this at a bolt (5.12b, crux) to another bolt, then mantle again to one more bolt, and slab climb (5.10d) left to a left-facing, left-arching corner (pin). Up this twenty feet, then pull over arch and face climb to a bolt and pin belay. 130', 5.12b

3. Step right to bolt, then up face and mantle (bolt) up to flakes. Climb flakes up steep wall to a stance and a bolt, then climb left to a shallow, left-facing corner. Up the corner to a bolt on the face. Step left (5.10d)

Steve Dupuis rests after hauling on Lowther Memorial   Sykes

to steep face climbing and one more bolt, over this to the Lab Wall amphitheater and belay at two bolts and a pin. 110', 5.10d

4. Traverse left to a steep, right-facing wall (bolt), climb past another bolt, then up to a large ledge and a roof above. Clip the bolt and pull over the first roof (5.10d) to one more bolt and the last roof. Climb through roof out right, and up an unprotected 5.9 R face to a two-bolt belay on the right. 100', 5.12b (5.9 R)

5. From belay, climb steep hollow flake (pin) to connect with Labyrinth Wall's fifth pitch after the traverse. 5.11

History: Jon Sykes and Bill Lowther completed the first three pitches in the summer of 1994. Sykes free climbed the second pitch with Mike Kenney in the summer of 1996. Sykes then worked on the fourth pitch with many partners trying to free a difficult section. Unsuccessful, Sykes finally aided this section with the help of Chuck Woodman on September 25, 1995, climbing through the amphitheater roof at 5.10d, 5.9 R A1. The first complete ascent of Meltdown to Lab Wall and the top was done on August 5-6, 1996, by Jon Sykes and Steve Dupuis. Tim Kemple and Pete Vintoniv freed pitch 4 at 5.12b on September 6, 1999.

★ Benedictus Direct IV 5.11d A3 [2 points of aid]

The original aid line now goes free, except for two points of aid on sky hooks on pitch 5. Bring a modern rack to 3″, including micro-wires. Double ropes are useful. Start on the top of a small buttress at a double-bolt anchor to the right of the horizontal ceiling at the base of Lab Wall Direct.

1. Climb a flake to a short left-facing corner. Layback the corner (5.11a, bolt), step left, then face climb up a series of flakes (5.8 R) to a large ledge. 85′, 5.11a, 5.8 R

2. Layback and face climb up to a beautiful finger crack (5.11a), slicing up the center of a clean steep face. Belay at a stance in an arch. 100′, 5.11a.

3. Climb the arch to its top. Belay on the right on a narrow ledge. 40′, 5.9 (Pitches 2 and 3 are often combined.)

4. Face climb right to a ramp system that leads back left to a right-facing flake. Climb the flake (5.11b, bolt) and belay on top of it at a triple-bolt anchor. 85′, 5.11b

5. Free climb (5.11d) or hook past three bolts to an overlap, then aid through the overlap (hooks), and free climb to a horizontal crack. Down climb left to a belay at the double-bolt anchor at the top of pitch 5 of Lab Wall. 90′, 5.11d A3

6. Climb up and right to the horizontal crack. Face climb right to a large overlap, 2 pitons (5.10b). Pull past the overlap on buckets (5.9+ R). Continue up the spectacular face to the next overlap and a two-bolt belay, or traverse right to a two-bolt belay on YMC Dike. 120′, 5.10, 5.9+ R

7.-8. Continue to the top on YMC Dike, or make three long rappels down to the ground.

Variation: Pitch 5a: 5.11c, 5.9 R

5a. This variation allows for a completely free ascent of Benedictus Direct. From the top of the flake, face climb left along a seam (5.9 R) to a stance at a bolt. Face climb left to a second bolt. Make difficult moves further left (5.11c) to join Pitch 5 of Walk on the Wild Side below the steep headwall. Overcome the headwall (also 5.11c), and belay on the same small ledge as for Pitch 5. 100′, 5.11c, 5.9 R

Pitches 6, 7 and 8. Same as for Benedictus Direct

Variation on Pitch 5b: Insult to Injury 5.12 A0, 5.9+ R

An amazing two-pitch variation that will go free with wild moves and exposure.

Pitch 5b. Begin at the triple-bolt belay on top of pitch 4. The crux pitch has not been red-pointed. From the top of the flake, face climb straight up a blank wall (5.11d) past three bolts to an overlap. Traverse right under the overlap, executing strenuous but delicate moves (5.12, bolts), to a rest in a flaring corner beneath another bolt. Finally, pull past the overlap (5.10d) to a double-bolt belay on a good ledge on the slab above. 75', 5.12 A0

Pitch 6b. Face climb off the left end of the ledge to a bolt. Make hard slab moves (5.10d), then run it out (5.9+ R) to a fixed piton in a horizontal crack. Step left, and run it out again (5.8 R) to a bolt, then face climb left along a horizontal crack (5.9 R) to a large overlap (2 pitons) and a junction with Pitch 6 of Benedictus Direct. Pull over the overlap at a bucket (5.9+ R), and continue up the face to the next overlap and a two-bolt belay. 120', 5.10d, 5.9 R

When I Paint My Masterpiece IV 5.11c

This climb is the culmination of many years of work by many people, combining a completely free ascent of Benedictus Direct with a direct finish. It is certainly one of the finest long free routes on the East Coast. It uses parts of Walk on the Wild Side and Labyrinth Wall Direct. The climb is similar in difficulty, character, and quality to Walk on the Wild Side, yet it is longer and more sustained. Double ropes recommended.

Pitches 1-6. Climb Benedictus Direct with the free variation (Pitch 5a) to the two bolt-belay at the overlap atop Pitch 6.

7. Traverse left, then up to a good crack below the overlap (5.9). Step right (bolt) and undercling (strenuous) over the overlap to another bolt 5.11b. Traverse right to a stance (bolt). Slab climb 5.10c up and left to a fourth bolt (5.9 R). Climb up the face and join Walk on the Wild Side for its last 20', traversing right (5.10a) to a belay with four bolts. 100', 5.11b, 5.9 R

8. Face climb straight up (5.9 R) to a bolt. Step left (5.10d) to a right-leaning arch (junction Lab Wall Direct). Climb this arch (5.9) to a belay with two bolts. 80', 5.10d, 5.9 R

9. Angle left to a dowel, face climb further left (5.9), then face climb back right (Lab Wall Direct goes left) and climb straight up the face past three bolts to the shrubs. (85', 5.10d) You can rappel from here, if desired, from small trees.

10. Climb up a dirty slab to a belay in the bushes. 140', 5.6

11. Scramble to the top through bushes; third class.

History: Howard Peterson rope-soloed the first three pitches of

Benedictus in October of 1974, intending it as a direct start to Labyrinth Wall. In the summer of 1975, Ed Webster and Stoney Middleton made the first ascent of the Benedictus/Lab Wall combination. Chris Ellms, Doug White, and Steve Schneider made the first free ascent of Benedictus in June of 1976. Bruce Bundy, Chris Kulczycki, and Steve Larsen completed the aid finish, Benedictus Direct, in 1984, after wandering off Lab Wall and getting Lost in the Ozone. The first pitch was altered by rock fall in 1992 and became much harder. It was re-led in July of 1992 by Tom Callaghan and Chris Dube, who also free-climbed pitch four (originally freed without the bolt by Dube). Later that same year, Callaghan and Dube also free-climbed pitch five, except for the two sky hook moves. Tom Callaghan and Mark Bowen finally made the first continuous free ascent of Benedictus Direct (with the two hook moves) in October of 1993. The first free ascent of the free variation (Pitch 5a) was done by Chris Dube and Tom Callaghan in July of 1993. Using this variation, Tom Callaghan, Fred Wiggins, and Paul Nager made a completely free ascent of Benedictus Direct in October of 1993. "Insult to Injury" was the result of numerous attempts by Tom Callaghan and Mark Bowen in 1994 and 1995 to free climb Benedictus Direct without using parts of Walk on the Wild Side. In October of 1995, they got close to a completely free ascent. The traverse above the 5.11d face has never been red-pointed. Tom Callaghan and Mark Bowen created "When I Paint My Masterpiece" in 1997 and 1998. A complete free ascent of Benedictus Direct with the "When I Paint..." direct finish, was accomplished in July of 1999 by Tom Callaghan, Mark Bowen, and Tom Nonnis.

YMC Dike IV 5.10 R

This is the vertical dike system you can see on the right side of the Big Wall. It is a demanding route with loose rock and poor protection. There is also an alternate start via Fruit Cup Wall that is more protected.

1. Climb easy, but loose rock in the dike to a belay stance. 80'

2. Climb up ten feet, traverse left under an overhang. Pull over on questionable rock, back right, then up a shallow corner. Traverse left (5.9) into the dike and up to a large, rotten cave.

3. Head around the right side of the cave and up a blocky dihedral. Step left into a right-facing dihedral, and climb it to a belay ledge on the left.

4. Above the cave, climb up the dike (5.8 R) to a belay stance on the right under an overlap.

5. Pull the roof (5.10 R) to moderate face climbing on good rock. Small belay stance below the next overlap.

6. Move up a left-facing corner and through the ceilings above (5.9+, old pins) and climb up and right to a ledge.

7. Climb to a ledge on the right, then back left on flakes into a U-shaped groove and climb easy rock to a big ledge.

8. Up the dike (5.8+) past two bolts to the top, or traverse right, then one short rappel to enter the Conn Gully.

History: The first ascent of the first three pitches was made by Sam Streibert, Phil Nelson, and Alan Wedgewood on October 12, 1964. John Reppy, Sam Streibert, and Bob Crawford took the route four more pitches on September 19, 1966. The first complete ascent was done in June, 1967 by Sam Streibert and Sandy Bill. Ed Webster and Dennis Goode free climbed the original aid sections on June 30, 1978. They used an alternate start up Fruit Cup Wall described below. The name of this route, YMC Dike, refers to the Yale Mountain Club.

Variation: The Alternate Start II 5.9+

1. & 2. Climb pitches one and two of Fruit Cup Wall. 5.9

3a. Up the third pitch of Fruit Cup Wall; undercling an arch left and surmount the overlap (5.9+). Up a crack system (5.6) and connect with the YMC Dike above the rotten cave. 5.9+

FA: Ed Webster and Dennis Goode June 29, 1978

★ Fruit Cup Wall V 5.11c (or 5.9+ A3)

Another Grade V big wall that has fallen to the free-climbing frenzy. The original climbing on pitch four, five, and six can still be aided. The route will be described in its original condition. The start is left and uphill from the Conn Buttress.

1. Climb through loose flakes and step right to a grassy corner. Move up to the base of the left of two left-facing corners and belay at a small stance.

2. Head right and climb a prominent, left-facing dihedral, then friction up a slab to bushes and belay. 5.9

3. Undercling left out an arch, and climb through an overlap (5.9+). Climb the crack system to a small belay. 5.9+

4. Face climb to a short bolt ladder that leads to a spacious but sloping bivi ledge. 5.9 A1

5. From the left side of the bivi ledge, climb a shallow, left-facing dihedral to the arch, and undercling it left (5.11c). Then climb up to a small belay stance. 5.11c (or A3)

6. Aid or free out right, then move left using thin pins until you can move straight up to a ledge. 5.11c R (or 5.7 A3)

7. From the right side of the ledge, free climb up to and jam a grassy crack up a large slab. This leads to a left-facing corner, then climb the corner up to and over a ceiling and belay. 120', 5.10c

8. Climb the face past bushes, and step left to a large ledge. Move up green wall, then hand traverse right and up to a belay ledge on the left. 120', 5.8

9. Ascend the face up to a layback crack and a sloping belay. 100', 5.8

10. Climb small holds on the face to a prominent corner. Move left and climb one more dihedral to the top.

History: The first ascent of this historic climb was completed by Peter Cole and Rick Wilcox on August 12 and 13, 1974. Ed Webster and Dennis Goode free climbed the first three pitches on June 29, 1978. In October, 1993, Steve Larson and Andy Tuthill free climbed pitches five and six without placing any new bolts on either pitch. Larson led the A3 pitch five and Tuthill took on the A4 pitch six. A few days later Brad White, Ian Cruickshank, and Paul Cormier freed a variation left of the bolt ladder on pitch four placing one bolt and a pin.

Andy Tuthill, Susan Frankenstein, and Steve Larson then attempted to free the entire route in the summer of 1995 making it to pitch 8 as their high point. Finally on September 11, 1995, Brad White and Paul Cormier completed the first free ascent of the entire route using a variation on pitch six. They climbed the entire route in a speedy seven hours.

Variation: Rainmaker 5.10c
This is a new, cleaner start to Fruit Cup Wall.

1a. Twenty feet left of the start to Moby Grape look for a pin leading up and right to a bolt on a friction face. Climb up to a bolt, then past another bolt that leads you up an arching ramp to a two-bolt belay. 5.10c

FA: Paul Cormier and Brad White Summer, 1999

Variation: Rainmaker 5.10c
2a. From the original first pitch belay, instead of traversing right, head straight up to a shallow but obvious left-facing corner capped by a roof. Climb the corner and pull out the roof to a two-bolt belay. 5.10c Intersect with Fruit Cup's third pitch.

FA: Brad White and Paul Cormier September, 1995

Variation: Easier Alternate Second Pitch 5.9
2b. From the first belay climb to the base of an inside corner facing left, but do not climb the corner. Traverse left past two bolts toward YMC Dike then a blocky left to the same belay as above. 5.9

FA: Paul Cormier and Brad White September, 1995

Free Variation: 5.11a

climbing the bolt ladder, climb out left past a bolt and a hid-
to the spacious bivi ledge and belay. 5.11a

te, Ian Cruickshank, and Paul Cormier October, 1993

Alternate Free Variation 5.11a

6a. From the belay, step down right and undercling 15 feet right to a left-
facing corner. Climb the corner past fixed pins, then face climb left until
you are above the last belay. Climb straight through overlaps above
(5.11a) past two bolts; the first bolt is hidden from view. Layback past
the second bolt and up to a belay ledge.

FA: Brad White and Paul Cormier September, 1995

Trojan Crack I 5.9

1. Climb the chimney off-width crack just left of the first pitch of Moby
Grape. 5.9

FA: Dave Anderson, Lindi McIlwaine, and Mike Kenney July 17, 1982

Sabwo Crack II 5.9

An awkward climb up the left side of the Conn Buttress.

1. Climb the first pitch of Moby Grape. 5.8

2. Stay in this crack, climbing to a flaring chimney and exit left to reach
the top of Conn Buttress. 5.9

FA: Paul Baird and Howard Peterson 1974

Pepe's Face I 5.11+ or 5.12-

The bolt-protected face just left of Reppy's Crack on the Conn Buttress.

1. Friction up the smooth face, and at the last bolt traverse right and into
a crack that leads to a two-bolt belay. 130', 5.11+/5.12-

FA: Rusty Reno 1980s

★ Moby Grape III 5.8

This route is probably the best alpine 5.8 on the East Coast and a must do
for any aspiring Cannon climber.

Start at the left edge of Conn Buttress 15' left of Reppy's Crack. Bring 4"
protection for first pitch.

1. Layback the awkward rounded crack 35' to a finger crack. At the top of
the crack step right and layback and jam the main corner to a break on
the right (crux). Step around right and diagonal up the front of the buttress. Belay at a pin. (145', 5.8) This pitch can be split.

2. Jam the 10' finger crack, then scramble to the top of the buttress. Belay on a ledge directly below the triangular roof. 150', 5.7

3. Up left, then step right to a beautiful finger crack and up to the triangular roof. Pull over its left side (strenuous 5.8). Follow easy cracks and flakes up right to the belay. 120', 5.8

4. Move right and diagonal across precarious blocks. Follow a right-leaning corner past an old peg. Then straight up clean, granite corners and cracks to a ledge with a slab on the right. 90', 5.7

5. Up the slab using the diagonal finger crack. Make a delicate step right and pull over the Sickle and up to the Finger of Fate. Climb squeeze chimney (left) or hand traverse from the right to the top of the Finger. Step across a 5.6 slab and up to a long, large grassy ledge. 100', 5.8

6. Walk left 35 feet to a dike and make a tricky bouldering move. Climb easy ledges trending right to another long ledge. 130', 5.7 (Escape right to the Conn Dike is possible from either P5 or P6 belay ledges.)

7. Climb the often-wet flakes above the belay. Up a ramp to a friction move (5.7) above a small, left-facing corner. Walk right to the large, left-facing corner. Move up to a cave and make a strenuous move out right. Climb the cracked slabs, moving diagonally right to a belay at a grassy ledge above a huge block. This pitch can be split if rope drag becomes a problem. 160', 5.7

8. Follow a right-trending crack system aiming for a point of rock on the skyline. Make a delicate slab move below parallel vertical cracks (sometimes wet). Jam the short cracks to exit cracks above (caution with rope jamming). 160', 5.6

FA: Joe Cote and Roger Martin July, 1972

History: There are two stories on how this route got its name. One says that the first ascent title came from the British rock group, Moby Grape, from the early 1970s. In the second story, Joe Cote was irritated by someone asking him what route he was going to climb while he was mixing up a batch of Moby Grape Koolade—hence the name. The Koolade flavor and the rock band are long since gone, but the climb remains.

★ Alternate Finish: Kurt's Corner I 5.7+

This is a nice finish up the beautiful, left-facing dihedral at the top of the cliff.

8a. From on top of the cave, climb up and left to the long, left-facing dihedral, up this until it ends and belay. 140', 5.7+

9a. Finish by climbing easy slabs and grassy ledges to the top.

FRA: Kurt Winkler and John Colebaugh October, 1986

Roger Martin
climbs the Sickle
on an early
ascent of Moby
Grape

Roger Martin

★ Reppy's Crack I 5.8

This is without a doubt the finest hand crack in the White Mountains.

1. Ascend the vertical jam crack on the front of the Conn Buttress up to and past the peapod (crux), to a sling belay (120', 5.8). Or climb past this into a corner on the right and up to a two-bolt belay on top of the Conn Buttress. 180' Alternatively, from the sling belay one can climb up and left in a shallow corner and up to the same two-bolt belay. 60-meter ropes are necessary for this variation.

History: Phil Nelson and Alan Wedgewood (UK) completed the first ascent on May 9, 1965, and named it in honor of John Reppy, who thought it would be a nice route.

Conn Course III 5.8

This truly historic route is seldom climbed. The V-groove on pitch four was destroyed by rock-fall in 1968. Moby Grape is now the preferred route to climb. Conn Course starts at the bottom of Conn Dike, just right of the Conn Buttress. Known as the Laundry Chute, this gully is very active with rockfall, so keep a mindful eye and ear open while moving through this zone.

1. Diagonal left up friction ramps past a block, ascend via body jamming. Climb up the gully's left side and belay below a corner. 150', 5.6
2. Climb down, then step left around the corner of the buttress, ascending a V-chimney part way. 120', 5.6
3. Move up through the rest of the V-chimney, and scramble (loose rock) to the top of the buttress.
4. Jam the finger crack and pull through the triangular roof on Moby Grape. The original route traverses up left and over blocks to a flared corner. (5.9/5.10) which leads to a sloping ledge. Friction up a ten-foot slab and traverse right fifty feet on a narrow ledge to where both lines converge.
5. Climb the fourth pitch of Moby Grape belaying on the higher of the two ledges. (See Moby Grape.) 5.8
6. Ascend up and left on slabs and little ledges, then friction back right to the bush-covered large ledge. 5.7
7. Traverse off right into Conn Dike and bushwhack up for 300 feet. Be careful with loose rock and granite gravel while in the dike.

History: Herb and Jan Conn made the historic first ascent on August 23, 1945. They wore tennis shoes and climbed the first major route up the middle of Cannon. This stands as a testament to their boldness and skill.

Psyche Dike III 5.9 R

This is the vertical dike system above the Conn Buttress. The start is just right of the buttress. Be prepared for route-finding difficulties and loose rock. Like other routes of dubious character, this is seldom climbed.

1. Climb the gully just right of Conn Buttress. Friction through a shallow chimney, up to blocks and belay below a right-facing corner. 140', 5.7
2. Step left and ascend the right-facing corner (King's Variation). Belay on a ledge left of the dike. 145', 5.7

Bill Keiler climbs the left variation of the Fickle Finger of Fate on Moby Grape

Jamie Cunningham

3. There is a rib just left of the dike. Climb the left side of the rib for fifteen feet, then step right and into the dike. Up the dike on easy ground, then past two overhangs to a belay ledge shared by Moby Grape and Conn Course. 140', 5.8

4. Climb thin flakes on your right to an overhang, then step left on Dead Man's Curve into the dike again. Layback a left-facing corner to an overhang and ascend poor rock to a ledge on the right. 150', 5.8

5. Climb through blocks, slabs, and flakes to a ledge. Traverse left, looking

A climber leads Reppy's Crack located on the front of Conn Buttress

Jamie Cunningham

for a dike above a dirty chimney. Up a steep corner to a belay on a ledge. 150', 5.7

6. Climb a flake up a slab to a ledge, then move left into the dike and make a boulder move up right to flakes. Climb the flakes, then back left and belay at the base of a groove. 150', 5.9 R

7. Climb the groove to a ledge, then through a chimney to a slab, and the top. 150', 5.5

History: Sam Streibert and Larry Winship completed the first ascent of the route in July, 1968.

King's Variation (the second pitch) was climbed by Harry King and partner in the 1960s as an alternate pitch to Conn Course. Dead Man's Curve got its name from Joe Cote and Ben Read after falling blocks almost ended their ascent in 1971.

★ Dolomite Wall   III 5.10

This is one of the more challenging and exposed free climbs on Cannon. Runouts, micro wires, and loose rock are the norm. The pull through the Shark's Fin roof is incredible, and it has great protection to back up the exposure. Like all Ellms and Tuthill routes on Cannon, Dolomite Wall is a very hard 5.10. These guys still don't know how hard they climb.

1. & 2. Climb the start of Psyche Dike, and move right into the rotten hole (the Bung Hole) and belay. 180', 5.7

3. Step left, and climb the yellow wall on small holds (pin) into a large V-groove. Climb this thirty feet then step left on steep face to a small belay stance. 100', 5.8

4. Climb up and left, then back right (unprotected) to a large, detached flake (bolt). Belay on a sloping ledge. 60', 5.9

5. Climb on top of the large detached flake, carefully. Up a thin crack system (hard 5.9) to the roof and the Shark's Fin. Climb out the fin and pull over the lip (hard 5.10) and onto a small belay stance.

6. & 7. Finish up left on Moby Grape or straight up at 5.8 R or off right up the Conn Dike (not recommended).

FA: Chris Ellms and Andy Tuthill May, 1978

November

Grade unknown, not recommended

Yes, there is a route that goes up the Bung Hole—the immense rotten hole of the Conn Dike just north of Conn Buttress. The route moves up the right side of the hole in some fashion.

FA: Peter Carman and Richard Millikan November, 1962

★ Encore   II 5.10

This route can be found just left of Claustrophobia. The first two pitches are the best climbing, and after that the rock gets a bit exciting with the usual wet, loose terrain found in this area.

1. Just right of the Laundry Chute (Conn Dike) is a set of left-facing arches. Up these arches to a belay spike and ledge on Claustrophobia. 5.10
2. Climb the left-facing corner above for forty feet, then up a broken wall (easy) to the old belay ledge on Union Jack's fourth pitch. 5.7
3. Ascend the dark wall to the left of a new two-bolt belay on top of Union Jack's fourth pitch. Face climb into the ominous overhangs, then follow the highest arch out left twenty feet. Layback up the arete—wild position. Climb to blocks and belay. 5.9+
4. & 5. Two more pitches of loose climbing can be yours, or you can rappel off with two ropes.

FA: Dave Anderson, Mike Kenney, and Lindi McIlwaine July, 1983

★ Claustrophobia III 5.10d (5.10a R)

Although this route wanders, it has high quality climbing, mostly 5.8 to 5.9. The crux is a one-move wonder.
1. Climb an easy left-facing corner for twenty feet to a finger crack in a dihedral. Up the crack system to a ledge and a pin belay (new) in the corner to your right. 5.8
2. Follow ramp up left to a slung spike (used for belaying on Encore's first pitch) past this and through an overlap to the older lower belay on Union Jack (big ledge). 5.10a R
3. Step right over Union Jack and face climb around an outside corner until below a large roof. Now layback down a few feet and make a hard reach into a hidden crack on the right. Pull over this and climb the crack to a small stance. 5.10d
4. Jam the main crack, then climb the hand crack on the right (variation around Half Moon Crack) to the belay above Half Moon Crack. 5.9
5. Follow Vertigo to the top, or make two rappels down Vertigo with two 60-meter ropes to the ground.

History: Ed Webster and Bryan Delaney did the first ascent of pitch three and four in the summer of 1975 as a direct finish to Vertigo. Chris Rowins and Chris Ellms completed the first ascent of the entire route in November, 1975.

★ Variation: Tip Trip I 5.11a

1a. Just right of the start of Claustrophobia is a mini-buttress with a thin crack running down the middle of the face. Climb crack and face to its top, then up the crack system on Claustrophobia's first pitch to a pin belay. 5.11a

FA: Unknown

★ Union Jack III 5.9 (5.7 R)

One of many Cannon classics on this section, Union Jack's second pitch is sweet, clean laybacking, and the fourth pitch's steep face and bomb-bay chimney will stop most 5.9 leaders. Start at a short hand crack on the face right of Claustrophobia.

1. Climb the hand crack system up to a short, right-diagonal crack. Hand traverse this to a belay stance. 100', 5.6
2. From the belay, ascend pockets up face to an overhang, then face climb left to the beautiful, left-facing corner. Up this, laybacking impeccable granite to a belay ledge. 5.9
3. Step right from the ledge and climb a thin, hollow flake past the large ledge on the left and continue up the face and corner to a two-bolt belay. 150', 5.8
4. Climb the steep face past a fixed pin and crumbly, side-pulling flakes (crux). Up to and through the bomb-bay chimney, and belay on huge blocks. 5.9, 5.7 R
5. Climb cracks on your left up to a steep crack on the right in a corner. Up this (tricky) to a large ledge and belay on your right. 5.7
6. **to 8.** Fourth and fifth class climbing through loose rock, bushes and slabs to the top. Alternatively, rappel down Vertigo; two raps with 60 meter ropes to the bottom.

History: The first ascent was done by Paul Ross and Ben and Marion Wintringham in June, 1973, using a small amount of aid. Michael Hartrich and Al Rubin established the "Old Glory Variation", by-passing the original aid section on pitch four a few weeks later.

Variation: Kehas' Korner I 5.9

3a. Climb the left-arching corners directly above the belay. 50', 5.9
FA: Dave Anderson and Andy Tuthill July 10, 1992

★ Vertigo III 5.9 A0 (one short pendulum)

The best 5.9 crack climb anywhere in the east. From fingers to hands to even body jamming in Half Moon Crack, Vertigo offers it all. The better start takes the first pitch of Union Jack or up the vegetated 5.5 corner to the right.

1. Climb the 5.5 corner or Union Jack's first pitch to a belay stance. 100', 5.5 or 5.6
2. Up pockets to an overhang and climb a striking thin flake system up and right (5.8) to a bolt. Lower off the bolt fifteen feet, then pendulum right

around a corner and climb a dihedral to a small belay stance.

3. Climb the stunning finger crack (5.9) and pull through the overlap to a belay ledge. 5.9

4. Make an exposed move out right, then climb a crack that widens from fingers to hand-size. Belay just below the Half Moon crack. (Pitch three and four can be combined.)

5. Grope, wedge, and slither up the notorious Half Moon off-width crack (5.9 R). (#5 cam will not work here.) A hard pull out of the off-width crack leads to a good belay ledge. 75', 5.9 R

6. Pull the overhang on the right, then up a corner. 5.6

7. Head left, a bit loose, then over a bulge to easy ground and the top.

History: John Bragg, Paul Ross, and Michael Peloquin completed the first ascent of the climb in July, 1971. John Bragg and Ajax Greene free climbed a couple of the upper pitches on August 10, 1973 starting up North-South-West. Pitch two was freed, except for the pendulum, in the spring of 1975 by Doug White and Tad Pheffer. In the summer of that same year Ed Webster and Tad Pheffer did the first continuous free ascent of the entire route using the pendulum on pitch two.

Variation: Crescent Moon I 5.9

A variation that avoids the notorious Half Moon crack.

5a. From the belay, climb to the fixed pin at the start of Half Moon Crack, then traverse left (5.9) into a left-facing dihedral. (You are now climbing the top of the fourth pitch of Claustrophobia.) Climb the corner to the overlap, and up the fingers-to-hands crack to the belay on Vertigo above Half Moon Crack. 5.9

History: Robert Miller and Scott Redtsma linked the two routes together in October, 1985, via the traverse from Half Moon to Claustrophobia.

Variation: The Bomb-Bay Corner II 5.10

Just right of Half Moon Crack is a left-facing bomb-bay dihedral. Climb the first two pitches of North-South-West and then prepare for judgment day.

3a. Layback up the thin dihedral to its top. 5.10

History: Dave Jones and Andy Tuthill did the first ascent with one point of aid (due to wetness) in the summer of 1979.

★ White Iceberg III 5.12b

Just left of North-South-West is a steep, bolt-protected face. Look for two bolts above a short right-facing corner. This is an awesome face climb with great protection.

Ken Reville leads
pitch three of
Vertigo

Jamie Cunningham

1. Climb the corner to a pin, then step left onto the steep face and work
your way past the two bolts (crux) and up to a large overlap. Pull the
overlap (pin) and climb to a two-bolt belay. 70', 5.12b

2. From the belay, climb up the steep face on down-sloping holds past several bolts leading into a shallow corner. Move through the corner (5.11d)
and up to the next bolt belay. 70', 5.11d

2a. You can avoid the 5.11d corner by stepping right into a short, dirty corner and up to the same belay. 5.11a

---

3. Move left a few feet to a large standing flake and climb up onto it. Now step back onto main face and follow a line of bolts up and right to the last belay in a corner. Rappel the route. 80', 5.10a

History: Jim Shimberg and Bradley White made the first ascent of the first two pitches using some aid on October 16, 1988. Shimberg rope-soloed the first complete ascent of the entire route two weeks later.

Shimberg then returned with Pete Gamache and free-climbed the second pitch in the spring of 1989. Scott Stevenson and Alan Cattabriga free-climbed the first pitch in November of 1989.

North-South-West III 5.9

This is one of the least-climbed routes on this section of the cliff. The first two pitches are vegetated and loose and unappealing. Look for the large, left-facing dihedral to the right of Vertigo.

1. Ascend the corner past a small overhang, and belay on the right. 80', 5.7
2. Forge up the corner and through a crumbly chimney and layback to bushes.
3. Standing below the huge slab, climb right to blocky overhangs.
4. From the overhangs, climb the thin crack on the left up the slab (5.9).

Irene Garvey makes the big reach on pitch four of Vertigo
Irene Garvey Collection

Head left, then down to a grassy ledge. 5.9

5. Follow the ledge left for fifty feet, and you should be above the Down East Slab. Climb the thin crack (pin) to easy ground.

6. & 7. Through the bushes straight up (bushwhacking), or up left near the Conn Dike and the top.

History: Phil Nelson, Sam Streibert, and Alan Wedgewood made the first ascent on August 1, 1964, intending to climb the large slab now climbed by Down East. A small section of aid on pitch four was free climbed by Henry Barber and Paul Ross during the first ascent of the Magical Mystery Tour in August, 1973.

★ Moonshadow III 5.9

A worthy outing with a stunning crux pitch up the arching dihedral right of Half Moon Crack on Vertigo. Begin 100 feet to the right of N-S-W, the same start as Down East. Look for twin, twenty-foot, left-facing corners.

1. Climb the corners up to the overhang, then undercling, traversing left 20' to a layback flake. Step up and exit right to belay level with a sharp pointed flake. 150', 5.7

2. Step down and left past flake into the left-facing dihedral. Climb the corner exiting right, then unprotected face climbing leads to a ledge. 110', 5.7

3. Easy climbing up and left to the base of the Down East Slab.

4. Head to the left end of the ledge, and step left into the left-facing corner—the stunning dihedral right of and parallel to Vertigo's Half Moon Crack—and layback to its top. 150', 5.9

5. Climb to the right, then back left continuing above the corner on good rock pulling over a short bulge split by a jam crack. 150', 5.8

6. & 7. Finish up and right to the summit.

FA: Al Long, Lindi McIlwaine, and Al Rubin May, 1976

★ Down East III 5.10a R

This route represents some of Cannon's best runout friction and testy crack climbing as well. The start is the same as Moonshadow. Look for twin, twenty-foot, left-facing corners.

1. Climb either corner, then step right and up another left-facing corner. Step right around an overhang to a belay ledge. 70', 5.7

2. Ascend a curving crack through a short wall. Move a little left to the next belay. 110', 5.9

3. Trend up and left to ledges at the base of a green slab. 100', 5.5

4. Climb a thin finger crack (5.9) that cuts through a small overlap eighty feet up. Belay ledge is on the right. 5.9

5. Ascend the low-angled finger crack, then traverse left and run it out up a clean slab trending left (5.10a R) to a ledge. The crux is at the end of the slab. 5.10a R

6. Step left, face climb to a corner, then mantle to the top.

FA: Jeff Pheasant, Michael Hartrich, and Al Rubin June, 1974

White Streaks of Trespass II 5.10

The start is thirty feet right of Down East.

1. Ascend dirty, crumbly rock up to the Down East belay ledge.

2. Traverse right ten feet and climb a hard twenty-foot crack to a belay on easy ground above. 5.10

3. Ascend higher on easy vegetated rock to Old Cannon Garden.

4. Climb the Indigo corner to the top. 5.8

FA: Chris Rowins, Chris Ellms, and Steve Schneider August, 1974

Shoebus Revenge III 5.11

This is another obscure route with the usual loose rock and route-finding problems that accompany this area of the cliff. Start roughly sixty feet right of Down East.

1. Climb a slab (5.6) to a corner, pull through an overhang, and head left twenty feet to the same belay ledge as Down East.

2. Ascend a hand crack on your right to its top. Step right up to a headwall (dowel). Climb up this on small holds (5.11), then up a hard slab (5.10+) at a thin left-leaning crack. Up a right-facing corner and belay. 5.11

3. & 4. Climb easy slabs and bushy ledges to the Down East Slab.

5. Layback up a right-facing corner on the right of the slab, then up a finger crack to a belay on the right. 90', 5.9

6. Continue up the finger crack (5.9), then easier climbing up left. Climb the face up past cracks and corners to the top.

History: Andy Tuthill, Dale Navish, and Chris Ellms climbed pitch five during the summer of 1978. The first complete ascent was done by Steve Chardon and Dave Jones on September 9, 1980, using one point of aid. Chris Rowins and Steve Schneider climbed the first free ascent in July, 1983. Rowins and Schneider were a formidable team on Cannon during the late 1970s and early 1980s.

Old Cannon III 5.6

Not recommended.

The historic first route up Cannon is unfortunately one of the more dangerous climbs due to repeated rock fall from above the Alpine Garden. Route-finding difficulties, loose rock, and hard-to-find protection are the norm. The start can be found two hundred feet left (south) of Wiessner's Buttress. Look for three parallel corners 200 feet above the ground.

1. Climb up broken rock, then through a right-facing V-groove hand jam and chimney up to ledges and belay on the left below a jutting roof. Look for a bolt and pin anchor that was still there in 1998. 110', 5.5
2. Head left, following grooves and shallow corners and continue left over spikes and loose flakes, then belay below the upper slabs. 140', 5.4
3. Move left on ledges until below a left-facing corner. 60'
4. Climb up the corner (pins) up to a ledge, then friction left into a gully, and up to a large vegetated ledge. Alternatively, one can climb up right following a loose left-facing corner with little protection and harder climbing.
5.–7. These pitches have been altered dramatically from recent rock fall. No route description is available.

History: After a first attempt on May 27, 1928, Robert L.M. Underhill and Lincoln O'Brien returned for the first complete ascent on September 18, 1928.

Due to the largest rock slide in the history of Cannon climbing, in the spring of 1997, the climbs starting with Old Cannon heading north to Wiessner's Buttress can not be recommended. Route descriptions for Blockade, Double Ganger, and Crack-up will not be given.

Blockade

Grade unknown. Not Recommended.

Double Ganger II 5.9 A1

Not Recommended.

Crack-Up III 5.9

Not Recommended.

The following two climbs ascend the face just left of what used to be Whaleback Crack. Torque and Whaleback Crack are now gone and everything below these climbs is now known as The Zone.

Indigo II 5.8

Amazingly, this climb survived the Whaleback rock slide. The safest way to reach this climb is via Wiessner's Dike to the Alpine Gardens. Then traverse south across The Zone (unprotected 5.2) for 400 feet to the base of a stacked buttress (two-bolt belay). There is very little protection on the traverse, and loose rock and gravel are found throughout The Zone. Care and common sense are needed here.

1. From the two-bolt belay, climb up left into a left-facing corner and belay on the right. 5.8

2. Follow cracks and bushwhacking to the top.

FA: Steve Chardon and Chris Rowins August, 1977

★ Whale Watchers II 5.9 (5.7 R)

This route is what's left of Torque and Whaleback Crack. Located on the right side of the buttress. The start is the same as Indigo at a two-bolt belay.

1. Head right from belay into the right-facing open book (5.7 R). Up this past pins to a flaring chimney (crux), then up the final chimney and a two-bolt belay on the right. 5.9 (5.7 R)

History: In 1972, Bob Anderson and Henry Barber completed the first ascent of Whaleback Crack establishing the first 5.10 on Cannon. Twenty-five years later, on June 19, 1997, that historic route came crashing down in the largest rock slide ever witnessed on Cannon. Just two weeks before, on June 8, 1997, Jon Sykes and Chris Marks made the last ascent of this notorious detached flake. On September 21, 1997, Jon Sykes, Gareth Slattery, and Mike Lee ventured out into the Zone for the first ascent of Whale Watchers. Do you dare?

★ Riddler III 5.9 or (5.12a)

There is definitely a riddle to this climb in older guides to Cannon. Here's my interpretation of the riddle. The start can be found fifty feet above and slightly south of the Old Man's Dog. Look for a ten-foot high, left-arching flake at the start of the upper wall. Segregation Flake will be one hundred feet directly above you.

1. From the belay, climb face and cracks up right to a belay in cracks twenty feet below the right side of Segregation Flake. You should be in the 5.8 dike. 80', 5.7

2. Slab climb up to a crack and overlap left of the right edge of Segregation

Flake. Move up the crack, then step right to the right edge of the flake. Up the corner to its top and belay at a two-pin anchor above and right of corner. 5.9 (You can combine the crack and face past two bolts for a more direct 5.12 pitch. **FA:** Tom Coe and Phil Brown Summer, 1989

3. Climb the left-facing corner to a small stance (old fixed wires). 60', 5.6

4. There are two possible ways up this section. The first is to climb directly up the corner to its end, then traverse hard left ten feet and pull through a roof. A lone 1/4" bolt and hanger will be just to your left after the roof. The other option is to traverse or diagonally face climb to the left of the overhang (5.8 R), up a short V-groove, and back right to the same bolt. Layback past the bolt, then traverse right twenty feet below huge stacked blocks (loose) and up a V-corner to a large vegetated ledge system. (You are now on the same ledge as the last pitch of Wiessner's Buttress.) 5.9, 5.7 R

5. There is no route description for this last section. One can either go directly up a steep broken wall in many different directions, all of them loose and uninviting, or head left on the ledge (bushwhacking) forty feet, then up broken corners to the top.

Henry Barber on the first ascent of Whaleback Crack in 1972
Bob Anderson, Henry Barber Collection

The author leads the
last ascent of
Whaleback Crack

Chris Marks

The author watches
for whales on the first
ascent of Whale
Watchers. Notice the
white outline above
the author—it's a
reminder of what used
to be Whaleback
Crack.

Mike Lee

FA: Howard Peterson and David Tibbetts July, 1972
FFA: Jeff Burns, Bryan Delaney, Howard Peterson, and David Tibbetts August, 1974

Variation #1: The 5.8 Dike I 5.8

The start is the same as Riddler; belay at the left-arching flake.

1a. Above the belay is the start of the 5.8 Dike. Climb face and cracks up and right into the dike. Ascend the right-leaning dike right of Segregation Flake. 5.8

FA: David Tibbetts and Chuck Zaikowski.

Variation #2: Little Jack's Corner II 5.8

1b. Climb the 5.8 Dike to a stance below the corner.

2b. Ascend the shallow, right-facing corner of Segregation Flake to its top, then step left into the belay above Segregation Flake. 130', 5.8

FA: Jeff Burns, David Tibbetts, and Howard Peterson Summer, 1974

Wiessner's Buttress III 5.6

Wiessner's Buttress is one of the oldest climbs in New Hampshire. Start below and left of the Old Man's Dog on a buttress. Climb the left side of the buttress in the corner.

1. Climb up the corner for 100 feet, then traverse left delicately under a small overlap (pins). 140', 5.6

2. Head left, then straight up loose rock to the Old Cannon Garden. 5.3

3. Walk right to the indented slab, and climb up the left side. 5.0

4. Climb right of a yellow, rotten dihedral, and ascend slabs to a belay. 5.5

5. Climb down a ramp on the right past a block. Make a big step to an inside corner, and climb it. Traverse right, slab climbing to a bush belay. 5.4

6. Descend right to the Archival Flake (also called the Hump), up this with much effort to the Classic Corner. Climb the corner to the top of the Old Man's Head and belay off cables. 5.6. (There is also a wonderful steep 5.7 face on the right wall of the last corner with great protection.)

FA: Robert L. M. Underhill and Fritz Wiessner 1933

Variation #1: Void Where Inhibited I 5.10b

A very exposed finale up the overhung prow just right of the last pitch of Wiessner's Buttress.

6a. Climb the left diagonal thin crack, then traverse right hand jamming a crack to a ledge. Move right around the corner and up the face to an

undercling right, and the top. 5.10b
FA: Dave Anderson and Chris Ellms July 18, 1982

Variation #2: The Right-Hand Dihedral I 5.8

When standing on the Lunch Ledge (see Lakeview), one can look up and see the right-hand dihedral just right 30 feet of Wiessner's finish. **WARNING:** Some of the cracks may be filled with silicone caulking to protect the Old Man's Head from the extreme weather in the Notch.

6b. From Lunch Ledge climb the alpine vegetation corner system up to the dihedral and the top of the Old Man's Head. 5.8

FA: Geoff Wood and Dave Isles

★ The Wag I 5.7+

Fifty feet left of Wiessner's Dike are bush-filled ledges. Bushwhack up to the higher of the two brushy ledges below hanging flakes.

1. Climb over stacked flakes to a stance below a hanging flake. Climb up past this very carefully (pin); yes, the hanging flake is loose. Follow thin vertical cracks (pins), traverse right 20' and climb a short flake to a ledge and a two-bolt belay on Wiessner's Dike. 120', 5.7+

2. From the belay climb left following the dike (loose), then pull through the dike and friction up to a lone bolt. Climb past the bolt and up a series of loose left-facing corners leading up the

Climber on the first pitch
of Wiessner's Buttress

Doug Teschner

left side of the Old Man's Dog. Belay at a two-bolt belay on top of the Old Man's Dog. Two rappels to the ground from here.

FA: Ed Webster and Kurt Winkler October, 1986

★ Variation: Fleabitten II 5.9 R A2

Climb the first pitch of The Wag and start at the (two-bolt) belay on Wiessner's Dike.

2a. Friction directly above the belay (5.9 R) past seams, then trend right five feet and up a thin crack. Move right to blocky corners, climb up these and step left into the corner of the Old Man's Dog and belay. 100', 5.9 R

3a. From the belay, down climb to under the roof and aid out the crack (fixed pins) to its end on the other side of the Dog's mouth. Free climb up horizontal cracks (5.8) and finish up the corners to your left (loose rock). 70', 5.8 A2

FA: Jon Sykes and Bill Kieler September 5, 1995

★ Variation: Beware of the Dog II 5.9

Gunks-like exposure on granite.

2b. Climb part way up the second pitch of Wiessner's Dike, traverse left and ascend a steep blocky wall to a ledge. Step left and belay in the corner of the Dog's Head.

3b. From the belay, traverse left out the Dog's jaw (exposed), then pull onto the nose. Traverse left (south) to the other side of the dog and climb horizontal cracks and loose flakes to the top of the Dog's Head and rappel from fixed anchor.

FA: Howard Peterson and David Tibbetts Mid 1970's

The Indented Slab

The Indented Slab sits between the upper pitches of Wiessner's Buttress and Wiessner's Dike, just above and right (north) of the Old Man's Dog. Two new routes can be found here along with a direct start completed on June 4, 2000. Look for a two-bolt belay at the bottom center of the Indented Slab. The direct start to Two Indented Heads Are Better Than One starts here.

★ Two Indented Heads Are Better Than One II 5.9

The original start began in the same left-facing corner of Wiessner's Dike as does Indented Servants but will be explained from the better direct start.

Bill Keiler cleaning
the third (crux)
pitch of Fleabitten
on the first ascent

Jon Sykes

1. From the bolt belay, climb past four bolts on moderate friction to the right (north) end of an overlap. Ascend the corner just right of the overlap to its end, then make thin (crux) moves left to a small left-facing corner; up this to another corner. Move over this to one final left-facing corner and the top. Two-bolt ring anchor. 160', 5.9

FA: Eric Pospesil and Jon Sykes October 16, 1999

FA: Direct Start: Jon Sykes and Gareth Slattery June 4, 2000

Indented Servants II 5.9

This route starts at the bottom of the left-facing corner of Wiessner's Dike above the Old Man's Dog.

1. From the corner climb out left and up to a bolt and a right-facing corner. Either climb up the corner (loose), or pull over the small overlap (crux) past the bolt and up to one more bolt. From here one can step left onto Two Indented Heads or follow the corner up to, and past a pin, and to the same belay as Indented Heads. 200', 5.9

FA: Jon Sykes and Eric Pospesil October 16, 1999

Wiessner's Dike III 5.6

This has become one of the classics on Cannon for moderately easy alpine climbing. Please be careful on loose rock and wear your helmet. Start at the prominent, fractured, left-diagonal dike below the Old Man's Dog.

1. Climb the dike up to a two-bolt belay. 130', 5.4

2. Step right and ascend blocky corners (pins), and past bushes trending right to a belay below the indented slab, fifty feet right of the Old Man's Dog. 140', 5.5

3. to 5. Move up the right side of the indented slab to reach a ledge at the base of a left-facing dihedral left of the Old Man. 5.3

6. Climb the dihedral, joining Lakeview in the middle of pitch seven. Ascend cracks and bulges to a belay at the base of a low angle slab. 5.5

7. Finish up the classic Wiessner's Buttress finish. 5.6

FA: Unknown

The Cannon Slabs

The classic Cannon Slabs have some of the most demanding friction climbs in the east. Route-finding is challenging here, and the climbing is varied, with cracks, overlaps, and of course the friction. From the easiest route, Lakeview (5.5) with its classic Old Cannon finish (5.6) on top of the Old Man of the Mountains, to routes like Consolation Prize (5.8), Falling Aspirations (5.8+), Odyssey (5.10), Condescender (5.11), and Cirrus (5.11), to the hardest route, Final Exam (5.11+), there are challenges for everyone on the slabs. Anyone climbing on the Slabs must watch out for rockfall from climbers on Lakeview. This route arches above the entire Slabs and is prone to rockfall from other climbers and after rain. Approach is from the climber parking lot in the north end of the Notch. (See page 19.)

★ Micron II 5.9

Begin 40' right of Wiessner's Dike.

1. Climb the prominent, left-leaning arch and belay at its end. 5.9

Climbers on Wiessner's Dike   Jamie Cunningham

2. Climb a ten-foot headwall, then head right using corners and cracks. 5.8
3. Finish up Wiessner's Dike.
FA: Steve Chardon, Dave Jones, and Chris Rowins August, 1977

★ Falling Aspirations III 5.8+

This is a great intermediate grade route, with fun and varied climbing. Originally, this route had several run-out (scary) sections for both leader and the second. Recently, several bolts have been added, and it is now considered to be a safe and enjoyable outing. This description deviates slightly from the original route on pitch two, making for a cleaner and dryer ascent, although it should be avoided immediately after a heavy rain.

Start 75 feet right of Wiessner's Dike, a large, left-facing arch which ends at the base of the cliff. Begin a bit right of this point.

1. Layback the middle of three small arches for 50 feet until you can move left to a finger crack leading to a small, right-facing corner. Delicately move around the corner and follow a ramp left past a bolt to a belay in a right-facing corner with two pegs. 130', 5.6
2. Climb the flakes above, then left and up two large holes, the second of which can be climbed on its left side avoiding the wet munge farther left. Above and left of the large hole, smaller holes and flakes head back

right and up to a low-angled slab beneath an overlap with a crack running through it. Climb the crack to a belay on the right at a good ledge with two old pegs deep in the corner. 135', 5.8

3. Move up to a bolt and climb the steepening slab up and right to a large right-facing corner. Follow the corner and flakes above to a belay at a nice ledge. 120', 5.8+

4. Move 30' right along a ledge and climb an insipient crack which widens then ends at a sloping ledge. Delicately step onto a detached block, and move up and right to a peg. Move straight up over the swell and follow finger cracks and flakes up to a friction move left to a good belay. 150', 5.7

5. From the belay, several friction moves lead up and right to a large corner on a low-angle slab. Where the corner arches leftward, break right and up to the low-angle slabs above and to a short vertical crack (old pin). Belay at the base of rotten flakes. 140', 5.4

6.-8. Follow Wiessner's to the summit.

History: In the summer of 1974 Chris Ellms and Steve Schneider climbed the first two pitches of the route. The direct start was also done with help from Howard Peterson that summer. Donna Coutu, Chris Rowins, and Steve Schneider completed the first ascent in the spring of 1976.

The author feeling small on the first pitch of Micron   Mike Lee

★ Variation: The Direct Start I 5.10

A heady pitch 50′ right of Wiessner's Dike.

1a. Climb the steep face past narrow flakes (pin) to the pin belay on pitch one of Falling Aspirations. 5.10

FA: Howard Peterson, Chris Ellms, and Steve Schneider Summer, 1974

★ Tales of Brave Ulysses II 5.10-

The title speaks well of the route. This is a strong lead not to be taken lightly. The crux pulls through the overlap on the second pitch.

1. Ascend with ease up to a belay ledge with a piton behind a flake. Above is a bolt below an overlap on the second pitch. 80′

2. Climb the slab above past the bolt and move through the overlap at a break on your right. Up right through a small arch, then step right once more and climb another arch, then past two bolts on a slab. Through one more overlap at an inverted "V" and belay to your right on Odyssey. 160′, 5.10-

History: Claude Muff and Ramsay Thomas made the first ascent in the traditional Franconia Notch style, placing all bolts on the lead in September, 1985.

Variation: Vindication I

(Still unfinished, grade unknown, but possibly 5.11+ or harder.)

1. Ascend up to the first bolt on Falling Aspirations, then follow line of old bolts up a blank wall.

FA: Jeff Burns and Chris Rowins early 1980s

★ Snooky II 5.8

This interesting route climbs the left-arching overlap 150′ right of Wiessner's Dike. Start on a ledge 15 feet up shared by Odyssey and Consolation Prize.

1. Climb the inside corner to a belay shared with Odyssey (bolts). 50′, 5.6

2. Layback up the Odyssey corner (very easy) and undercling left following the arch. Down climb 10′ on grassy holds and belay on small ledges. 100′, 5.8

3. Follow a line of ramps and ledges up left to a belay at the large spike shared with Falling Aspirations. Step left to join Wiessner's Dike. 150′, 5.5

FA: Steve Schneider, Chris Rowins, and Sam Pratt August, 1974

Variation: (Untitled) I 5.11+

Between Tales of Brave Ulysses and Snooky is a bolt- and pin-protected slab following an arete.

1. Climb the slab with difficulty to its end and belay at the end of Snooky's second pitch. 5.11+

FA: Rusty Reno (a California slab climber) Mid 1980s

★ Odyssey of an Artichoke III 5.10

The best 5.10 friction on the slabs of Cannon. Start on the same ledge as for Snooky and Consolation Prize.

1. Ascend Consolation Prize ramp for 30', then jam and layback the 4" to 6" crack up left to a good ledge (two bolts). 60', 5.7

2. Layback with ease up the arch for 35', then pull through the overlap (pin). Now the Odyssey begins by delicately climbing left (loose flakes), then up past two bolts on thin friction up to a two-bolt belay at a small ledge. 100', 5.10

3. Move right up the overlap, and pull over it at the corner. Climb over several small overlaps for 60' to a bolt, then up left to one more bolt and friction up a short slab (5.9). Head up left and belay at the base of a layback flake. 140', 5.9

4. Climb the flake, then right and up a short corner to an overlap. Ascend the thin crack past the overlap and belay at the base of a sweeping slab. 100', 5.8

5. Diagonal right up the slab, then back left under a small overlap to bushes and Lunch Ledge. 100', 5.6

6. Finish as desired.

FA: Chris Ellms, Chris Rowins, and Steve Schneider August, 1974
FFA: Jeff Burns, Stoney Middleton, and Steve Schneider Summer, 1975

★ Consolation Prize III 5.8 (5.2 R)

Yet another Cannon classic that weaves its way up the Slabs' highest section. Recent rockfall has altered the first pitch from 5.4 to 5.7, and the third pitch from 5.7 to 5.8. Begin at fallen blocks at the base of Condescender.

1. Scramble left up a ramp to a left-facing corner. Step up to a 6' horizontal crack and move right into a corner. Climb the corner/groove for 40' and belay at the first area of broken rock. 110', 5.7

2. Step down to a narrow ramp and move out right to its end. Move right with difficulty and climb the beautiful, right-slanting finger crack (crux) to a ledge. Ascend a right-facing corner (often wet) to questionable blocks. Move down left to a narrow belay stance (bolts). 120', 5.8

3. Move left and climb a staircase of holds (5.2 R) to an overlap (pins). Continue up friable slabs and small overlaps. Surmount the large overlap at a break on the right (pin-protected, tricky mantle). Trend right up to a two-bolt belay. 110', 5.8 (5.2 R)

4. Climb flaky rock (5.2 R) slightly left toward a vegetated corner (often wet). Avoid the loose blocks and move left along a horizontal crack to a small, left-facing corner. Up this corner to a two-bolt belay above loose blocks. 105', 5.5 (5.2 R)

5. Move up the easy, right-facing corner above the belay. Step left, then trend right, up slab to hidden holds. Follow weaknesses left and finish up a 10' finger crack. Belay in the bushes. 130', 5.7

6.-9. Join Lakeview on the right or follow a runway left (90', Class 3) to join Wiessner's. Approximately 250' to the large ledge below the Old Man.

History: Tom Lyman and partner climbed the first two pitches. Al Rubin and John Waterman climbed the first complete ascent on May 9, 1970.

★ Variation: Slabs of Lethe I 5.9

3a. From the belay head right, then climb straight up and past two bolts on a slab, and pull over the overlap and climb to the two-bolt belay on Consolation Prize.

FA: Tom Lyman and Danny Wilkins 1971

★ Variation: Connection I 5.8

This avoids loose rock on pitch 4 of Consolation Prize and provides a safe and interesting finish.

4a. From the belay at the end of Consolation Prize's 3rd pitch, diagonal up and right over a bulge to a bolt. Right to a pin, then delicate friction left (5.7) and up to a large overlap with a pointed thin flake at its lip (5.8). Move left around another overlap and climb up slabs to a belay at a horizontal crack. 150', 5.8

5a. Follow the Z-crack up and right to the belay at the end of Lakeview's 4th pitch. 60', 5.4

FA: Stony Middleton and Jed Eliades June 13, 1997

★ Condescender I 5.11a

This exceptionally thin, striking face climb is the best 5.11 on the Slabs. Start at fallen blocks just right of a short, right-facing corner. (The Consolation Prize start.)

1. Thin 5.11 friction off the ground past a bolt to a sloping, horizontal ramp (bolt). Step right and climb a shallow, left-arching open book past a bolt to a right, diagonal flake. Up the flake and face trending left to Consolation Prize's first belay in the first shattered rock. 140', 5.11

2. Climb up past the higher shattered hole and friction past two bolts on your left (south) curving back to Consolation Prize in the middle of the third pitch. 150', 5.9

History: Howard Peterson and David Tibbetts completed the first ascent of the crux pitch in July, 1977. Jeff Burns and Steve Schneider added the second pitch a few days later. (The second pitch is runout and sees very little traffic, probably due to the original quarter-inch bolts.) The bolts on pitch one were placed on rappel.

★ Variation: Condescending I 5.9+

Starting at the second pitch of Condescender is a line of bolts leading directly to the second pitch belay of Consolation Prize.

2a. From the higher shattered hole, step right following four bolts with the crux at the end and belay at Consolation Prize.

History: Although this face has been top-roped many times over the years, it has never been led until recently. Jon Sykes, belayed by Eric Carpenter, led the route on October 23, 2000, placing all the bolts on the lead.

★ Cirrus I 5.11b

There is a story behind this bold climb. The original start of this climb was not documented in Webster's 1986 guide book. John Strand assumed that the arete start had not been climbed and placed a bolt down low from a hook, and another bolt at the stance. He then led the climb, naming it Put Your Hands On Me, in 1988. On the first ascent, Chris Ellms bouldered up the arete with no protection to where the only pin on the route was placed. Start just left of Horrifying Ear.

1. From the ground, boulder up the arete to a bolt and a stance. Or climb up Horrifying Ear for twenty feet, then step left to the same bolt. From the bolt, face climb left and up to a pin. Climb the extremely thin crack up to Consolation Prize's second belay. 5.11b

FA: Chris Ellms and Mike Keating May, 1986

★ The Horrifying Ear (a.k.a. Eypper-Winship Slabs) II 5.9

Look for the hard-to-miss, wide chimney as you approach the base of the cliff from the north-end talus slope via the Consolation Prize approach trail (see map). Typically, climbers ascend the first two pitches, then combine with Consolation Prize at the second belay. The original route wanders across Consolation Prize and Condescender for two more pitches.

1. Layback up the right-facing corner and belay in the main chimney. 50', 5.5

2. Climb up the gaping chimney to its end, and pull over onto the face on the left (south). Ascend face up and left to Consolation Prize's second belay. 120', 5.8

3. Continue up Consolation Prize over the first overlap, then traverse left 30' along a thin crack joining Odyssey. Climb up to a small ledge with a bolt. 140', 5.7

4. Move left and up to another bolt, and climb the short slab (5.9). Move right under an overlap and scramble up to easier ground. 150', 5.9

FA: George Eypper and Larry Winship 1970

Ben Savage leads the mega-classic Condescender

Jamie Cunningham

Stoney's Revenge II 5.10 (5.8 R)

Ascend the bolt-protected slab between The Horrifying Ear and Vendetta. Look five feet right of The Horrifying Ear for a small corner/flake to start.

1. Layback up the corner/flake and belay. 60', 5.6

2. Face climb up and right (5.9) past two bolts, then friction up a hard slab to a thin, vertical fracture. Up this (5.10) into a hole (bolt), and then step down and right and belay at the top of the first pitch of Vendetta. 5.10

3. Climb up Vendetta for 15 feet, then traverse left thirty feet (5.8), up and right making 5.10 moves past a bolt and dowel, then continue (5.8 R) to the belay above on Slabs of Lethe. 5.10 (5.8 R)

4. Finish up Slabs of Lethe. 5.9

History: Chris Ellms and Stoney Middleton completed the route in the summer of 1980—ground up, notch style.

★ Vendetta II 5.9+ (5.7 R)

This route has seen recent rock fall. A section of overlap stretching from the second belay on Vendetta and ending at Slip-O-Fools' second belay station fell to the ground, destroying both belays. Other bolts on Final Exam, Stairway to Heaven, and Slip-O-Fools have been damaged as well. The first two pitches of Vendetta are now climbable; pins were replaced on the second pitch overlap and a two-bolt ring anchor replaces the destroyed belay on the second pitch. There is an unprotected slab now starting the third pitch. Start at the second, larger corner 15' right of Horrifying Ear.

1. Climb the corner (easy) then jam and undercling the large overlap out right to its end. Pull over on good holds and belay on your left. 120', 5.8

2. Climb directly above belay up a shallow corner system to the left end of a double overlap. Pull up onto smaller overlap above the larger one and traverse right past three pins to a two-bolt belay. 100', 5.9+

3. Climb a runout slab up to large overlap and pull over it at a weakness, then climb easy rock to a belay. 150', 5.7 R Finish on Lakeview.

FA: Peter Chadwick and Howard Peterson August, 1974

Final Exam II 5.11+

Seldom climbed, this route on the Slabs has seen recent damage to its bolts on the second pitch. Although they are all there, they appear bent and in bad shape. Start ten feet right of Vendetta at a vague ramp at the bottom of the slab below a large overlap.

1. Climb the ramp (unprotected) and pull overlap at a bolt (5.10+). Up to top of a flake, step left and undercling to Vendetta's first belay. 5.10+

2. From the right end of the ledge, friction past three bolts (very difficult) to an overlap (pin). Over this to Vendetta's second belay. 5.11+

History: This is one of very few rappel-bolted routes on Cannon. It took two attempts in July, 1984 for Carlton Schneider, Carrick Eggleston, and Kelly Bishop to complete the route.

★ Stairway to Heaven II 5.10

Jeff Burns' slab-climbing ability will impress you when you delicately friction up this gem. Start eighty feet right of Vendetta at a bolt fifteen feet off the ground.

1. Start directly below the bolt, or fifteen right. Climb past the bolt, then right to grass clumps. Follow sloping foot holds left, then up to large overlap. Traverse right 10' and make a hard move over the overlap to a bolt belay. 80', 5.10

2. Friction up the steep slab to a small hole (bolt). Continue up the slab past a tiny ledge (bolt), and pull through the overlap to a two-bolt belay on Vendetta's second pitch. 120', 5.10

FA: Jeff Burns, Chris Ellms, and Howard Peterson October, 1976

★ Slip-O-Fools II 5.10a (5.8 R)

This route has everything from thin crack climbing, to delicate friction, to tricky overlaps. Pitch two belay has just one bolt due to recent rock fall and the second bolt on pitch two is bent. Most parties climb just the first two pitches due to the lack of protection above the second belay. Start twenty feet right of Stairway to Heaven at a thin vertical crack.

1. Climb the crack and face (5.10a) or easier on the left up to a bolt. Pull over a tricky, shallow overlap and up to the next larger overlap. Over this at an obvious break to a semi-hanging belay. 80', 5.10a

2. Ascend the beautiful, clean slab above, past two bolts, and climb up a small corner (pin). Up the face past a small overlap, then up to a semi-hanging belay (one bolt) below a larger overlap. 80', 5.9

3. Make tricky moves pulling the overlap, then delicately traverse left above the overlap's edge (5.8-). Diagonal right (pins), then up to a belay under an overlap. 5.8 R (Caution: I have yet to find any of these pins on this pitch, making it very runout.)

4. Climb the arch above to its left end (5.7+), step over it and belay at blocks. 5.7+

5. Move up and right past several horizontal cracks, then climb over an overlap via a finger crack. 5.8

6. & 7. Finish on Lakeview.

History: Pitches one and two were done by John Mallery, Martin Mock, Mark Champagne, and Tom Callaghan in July, 1981. The entire route was completed on August 29, 1981 by John Mallery, Tom Callaghan, and John Strand. All bolts placed on the lead.

Lima Bean II 5.8

A rarely climbed route. Some twenty feet right of Slip-O-Fools, and one hundred feet off the ground, is a lima bean shaped depression. Start below this.

1. Climb past bushes 40', then traverse left on hard friction to a stairway of good holds. Up to a small overlap, step right and climb delicately (now bolt-protected) up a watercourse to the Lima Bean. 100', 5.8

2. Ascend directly above belay through some broken rock up to the large overlap. Pull overlap at a break—Slip-O-Fool's second belay is directly to your left—and climb the fun face above to a bushy ledge. 150', 5.7

3. Continue above to intersect with Lakeview's fourth pitch. 60', 5.6

FA: Howard Peterson, John Porter, and David Tibbetts June, 1972

★ Searching My Soul in a 3/8 Hole I 5.9

The start is located thirty feet right of Lima Bean. Look for an easy slab that meets a large upright boulder on the ground and start here.

1. Ascend easy slab up to a small overlap capped by a right-facing flake. Pull through the overlap here, then climb diagonally left to a larger overlap with a small, right-facing corner. Up through the corner (tricky) to a stance and follow right-facing shallow corners up to a bolt. Friction past this into another shallow right-facing corner (pin). Step left and mantle onto a stance in the Lima Bean watercourse (bolt). Climb up the watercourse and belay in the Lima Bean. Bolt and pin belay allows a speedy rappel with one 60-meter rope, or finish by climbing Lima Bean/Lakeview to the top.

History: Jon Sykes rope-soloed the route, placing the bolts free on lead on October 24, 1995. (I spent more than an hour trying to decide on the last bolt in the Lima Bean water course, hence the name.)

★ The Hold II 5.9+ (5.9 R)

Aptly named, this fine route is a hoot trying to figure out the moves past the hold. I highly recommend it. Start ten feet right of Searching My Soul in a 3/8 Hole. All bolts were placed free on the lead.

1. Face climb up a slab (bolt) to an overlap (past a bolt), move left and mantle (5.9+) over the overlap; then delicate friction takes you to a hole and a two-bolt belay. 90', 5.9+

2. Climb the slab above (5.9 R) to a large overlap. Move through this and zigzag through more overlaps and belay above. 5.9 R

3 & 4. Finish on Lyma Bean/Lakeview.

FA: Chris Ellms and John Powell June, 1986

FFA: Chris Ellms and Mike Keating April 26, 1987

Silly Putty II 5.7

Just trying to find this climb is the crux. Start roughly twenty feet left (south) of Lakeview.

1. Climb past two clumps of bushes and pull over three bulges and belay at bushes below an overlap. 150', 5.6

2. Pull the overlap, then diagonal up left on small holds and friction to a spike. Traverse left to a dike and follow it to a grassy belay. 150', 5.7

3. Move past small loose flakes and pull over the overlap where a small line diagonals up right on the downward facing end. 150', 5.7

4. Join Lakeview to the top.

FA: Howard Peterson, Dave Tibbetts, and Heidi Hamm June, 1972

Lakeview (Original) II 5.7

This route, like many others, has seen its share of rockfall. In 1962, a large section of rock on pitch two fell to the ground. The next year, Whipple and Andrews climbed the new slab in mountain boots, a hard 5.7 friction pitch by present standards. Unfortunately, this route is rarely done, replaced by the easier, newer Lakeview. Start at the first pitch of Silly Putty.

1. Climb past two clumps of bushes and pull over three bulges and belay at bushes below an overlap. 150', 5.6

2. Pull the overlap, moving up and right on the new slab. Belay at an obvious detached flake. 130', 5.7

3. Climb straight above you, then move left to a rock-filled crack. 150', 5.7

4. Friction up to a rounded flake and connect with the newer Lakeview. 100' 5.5

FA: Earle Whipple and Brad Giddings May, 1960

★ Lakeview III 5.5 (Wiessner's Buttress Finish, 5.6)

Start at an indistinct, left-facing corner system 100' south of the blocky outcrops at the extreme north end of the cliff.

1. Climb about 75' in the corner, then step up right and layback a clean 20' corner. Easy rock to a belay at the base of a prominent left-leaning arch. 140', 5.3

2. Use a 10' finger crack on the right to access the short corner above. Over the overlap, follow a horizontal crack out left. Step down, then follow a widening crack to a belay at its end (pin). 140', 5.4

3. Friction left 10' and pull over the overlap at a pin. Follow a curving finger crack left and up to a bulge. Friction over the bulge and walk left up an easy ramp. 160', 5.5

4. Continue traversing over bushes and easy ledges to a comfortable dirt ledge below a right-facing corner. 140', 5.2

5. Climb the corner slab to blocks above. Diagonal up left over outcrops and through bushes. 140', 5.3 (An earlier route goes straight up the path through the scrub.)

6. Make a tricky bouldering move in a short "V", or bypass it in bushes on the right. Scramble to the Lunch Ledge below the Old Man. 90', 5.0

7. Up the rotten gully 15', then diagonal out left across the clean face. Climb cracks and bulges to a belay at the base of a low angle slab. 80', 5.5

8. Friction up the slab to a large flake on the right. Struggle up the Archival Flake and climb the classic dihedral above to the Old Man's cables. 90', 5.6

FA: Dan Broiden, Roger Damon, and Andy Fisher April, 1962

A climber leads the second pitch of Lakeview   Doug Teschner

Good to the Last Drop II 5.7

Climbs the two obvious flakes on the face, 80' to the right of the Old Man's Profile. The climb is alpine in nature so there are no established belays. Belay just below the flakes.

1. Depart from Lakeview at an inside corner directly beneath the flakes. Climb to a stance 15' below the flakes. 100'
2. Move up on the right hand side of the stance for eight feet, then traverse left on the lower of two small ledges to gain the first flake. Climb the flakes to the top. 70'

FA: Paul Cormier and Jeff Campbell June 8, 1988

It should be noted that climbing the Old Man is illegal. This route is quite a ways to the right of the Profile.

The Little Prune II 5.7

The girdle traverse of the Slabs.

1. Start up the easier Lakeview, then traverse left to the first pitch belay ledge of the original Lakeview.
2. Climb up and left, traversing to Lima Bean and belay.
3. Keep traversing left and belay at Vendetta.
4. Finish by climbing Consolation Prize.

FA: Howard Peterson and Bob Rittenhouse June, 1974

Magical Mystery Tour IV 5.9

The north to south girdle traverse of Cannon is most likely the longest roped climb in the east. The first ascent party traversed 6,000 feet in just under six hours. A blistering pace to say the least.

Climb pitches 1 through 4 of Lakeview and move left to join Wiessner's. Down climb Wiessner's to Old Cannon Garden, then traverse left across the garden to its end at North-South-West. Up N-S-W and climb its difficult crack pitch. Traverse left; it's mostly easy ground, yet has some difficult sections. Climb into the rotten Conn Dike, move up the gully for two pitches, and traverse left along a ledge system. This section is vague but keep working left as far as possible, then rappel 165' to the top of the fifth pitch of Labyrinth Wall. Difficult climbing straight left brings you to the long flake that slices across the entire big wall. Traverse across this unique flake to its extreme left end (top of pitch 5 of Ghost). Climb up and left (5.7) joining Sam's Swan Song; follow it to the top of pitch four. Climb left two pitches to the second Cow Pasture on top of the Duet Buttress. Down climb a gully to the first Cow Pasture and traverse straight left

Mike Severino on
the classic
Lakeview

Doug Teschner

(150'), to Cannonade. Down climb Cannonade to the top of Cannonade
Buttress. Traverse left on top of the buttress to the Black Dike. Down climb
until a traverse just above the gully base brings you to a 100' corner and
crack that leads to the Whitney-Gilman Ridge. Finish by climbing the
ridge.

FA: Henry Barber and Paul Ross August, 1973

The Reverse Girdle IV 5.10

The South to North girdle of Cannon is equally significant.

Chris Ellms and Andy Tuthill completed a reverse girdle in the summer of 1976, following in reverse Magical Mystery Tour until the Big Wall. When Sam's Swan Song is reached, one must down climb to the top of Triple S Buttress. Face climb up and right (5.9) to reach Labyrinth Wall, then continue to friction right to the YMC Dike (5.10). Diagonal up and right, joining Moby Grape. At the top of the fourth pitch of Moby Grape, traverse right under an overhang and join Magical Mystery Tour at the Conn Dike. Finish via the Old Man.

A true, complete girdle traverse still has not been done. There is about a thousand feet of traverse from the Whitney-Gilman Ridge heading south to the Henderson Buttress left to climb. Unfortunately, you must climb over and through some of the loosest rock on Cannon, so please exercise great caution when attempting this.

Attention: The Bubba Marty and Cheek to Cheek, both located on the Old Man's Head, are now closed to climbing. Both routes' cracks have been filled with waterproof sealant to protect the Old Man's Head from the ravages of winter.

A climber struggles over the Archival (The Hump)—the finish to Wiessner's Buttress and many other routes that end on the Slabs

Doug Teschner

Artist's Bluff

School groups and camps have long used Artist's Bluff and Little Monalisa, 200' and 60' high respectively, as a training ground. These two small cliffs stand at the north end of Franconia Notch with wonderful views of the surrounding peaks. The approach is easy: from Echo Lake parking lot on Route 18, walk east about 100 yards to the Artist's Bluff hiker's trail. Follow this trail for 150 yards to where the base of the larger cliff is visible on the right.

The smaller cliff, Little Monalisa, is higher up, above a gully just left of the trail. Little Monalisa is characterized by good beginner face routes. An easy line left of center (5.2) follows a left-slanting dihedral, then back right and more or less straight up the white cross in the center of the cliff. A more direct version, bypassing the dihedral, is 5.4.

Another easy line (5.3) goes up and out to the right along a diagonal crack, then back left to the top. Closer to the trail, a more challenging line (5.6) follows a steep crack eventually connecting with the right-diagonal crack route. More challenging face climbs can be found between these three major lines.

The top of the small cliff is reached by following the hiking trail. Go left on the trail toward Bald Mountain, past the side trail to the top of the main cliff. When the trail enters the woods, go left on an obscure climber's trail to the top of the small cliff and a two-bolt belay.

The larger cliff has three major top-to-bottom lines with numerous variations in between. Routes are described from left to right. The top of the Cliff is reached easily by following the hiker's trail.

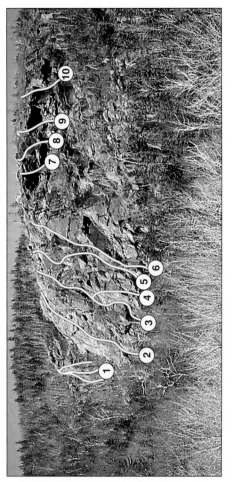

Route listing for Artist's Bluff

1. Little Monalisa with routes from 5.2 to 5.6
2. Standard Route 5.5
3. Brass Balls 5.8
4. Handy Cap Direct 5.12
5. Special Olympics 5.10c
6. Right Side Route 5.6

(7 through 10 are unnamed)
7. 5.9+
8. 5.7
9. 5.7
10. 5.6

★ Standard Route I 5.5

This route, the most popular at Artist's Bluff, starts in the obvious large corner on the cliff's left side.

1. Climb up into the corner on down-sloping holds (harder than it looks) and up an obvious corner to a ledge on the left. 50', 5.5

2. Traverse 15 feet right along large ledge, then up the steep face above following the path of least resistance (many variations). 100', 5.3 to 5.5

Variation: Standard Direct I 5.6

1a. Fifteen feet right is a direct start to Standard Route. Look for a lone pin below a blocky corner.

★ Variation I 5.7

2a. Climb the bulge directly above the belay ledge via a finger crack and continue up the face above. 110', 5.7

★ Variation I 5.10a

3a. Just left of the finger crack is another harder 5.10a finger crack that leads you to easy face climbing and the top. 110', 5.10a

★ Brass Balls I 5.8

One of the best routes at Artist's, with a sustained crux pitch. Start in the obvious inside corner, below a tree, 50' right of Standard Route. Microwires, offsets, and tiny cam units (TCUs) are needed.

1. Climb up the corner to a tree. 30', 5.6

2. Thin and exposed traverse right, then up the face above to easier ground. Near the top, it is possible to exit left up an easy corner. A better finish is the right diagonal crack up a steep wall to an exciting finish. 130', 5.8

Variations:

There are two 5.10 variations directly above the first pitch belay tree, and there is a 5.11 variation through the roof on the left, led by Mike Zamicky in 1979.

★ Handy Cap Direct I 5.12a

1. Follow the line of bolts directly up through a slightly overhung face to a two-bolt belay.

FA: John Mallery and Chris Rowins 1989

Chris Marks leads the perplexing Special Olympics

Jon Sykes

★ Special Olympics I 5.10c

1. Climb diagonally right past four bolts to a natural belay in a horizontal crack. The two-bolt belay on Handy Cap Direct is up and left.

FA: John Mallery and Chris Rowins Spring 1989

History: Rowins hobbled into Artist's Bluff on crutches that day and seconded both routes with no falls. Now that's moxie.

★ Right Side Route I 5.6

This route starts 75' further to the right (and slightly down) from a short, left-facing corner.

1. Climb up corner, out right and up a nice off-width crack to a belay on a low-angled slab. 75', 5.6

2. Continue up easy slab and corner to an alcove. Climb up left following cracks and blocks to a bulge, which is climbed (possible variation left on vegetation-filled foot traverse) to the ridge. Easier climbing over blocks leads to the top. 120', 5.5

★ Artist's Arete I 5.5

2a. Climb down slightly from the belay ledge and head out left and up the arete above. 130', 5.5

Chris Marks cleans the wax out of Vincent's Ear on the second ascent

Jon Sykes

★ Diagonal I 5.3

2b. Follow ramp in regular route but instead of surmounting the bulge, head right and slightly down on vegetation to a major bushy ledge under an overhanging wall.

3b. A nice path on beautiful rock. Climb face via flakes to gain left diagonal, traverse right and follow it to the top. 60', 5.3

The overhangs on the upper far right (north) side have four short routes worth mentioning. Starting from the left is a diagonal crack system rated 5.9+, two 5.7's to the right, and a 5.6 on the far right side.

On the lower far right side of the main cliff are three short routes worth checking out. Follow the trail along the base of Artist's Bluff heading north past the Right Side Route 100 yards to the start of Vincent's Ear and The Corner.

★ Vincent's Ear I 5.10c

Look for the short, beautiful two-bolt arete.

1. Make gymnastic moves off the ground past the first bolt (crux). Continue up to the second bolt past horizontal cracks and the top. Belay with natural gear, then walk off. 50', 5.10c

FA: Jon Sykes and Jamie Cunningham August 2, 1996

The Corner I 5.10c X

This is the obvious, right-facing dihedral capped by a bulge. It used to have a pin halfway up the corner that pulled when a student at the White Mountain School fell, while trying to lead the route. Luckily, he walked away with minor injuries.

1. Climb the corner to its end, then move right, underclinging a crumbly flake. Make hard moves into (crux) and up the corner with no protection to the top. Belay off natural gear. 50', 5.10c X

FA: Alan Pilgrim and partner Late 1980s
FFA: Jon Sykes and Tim Burke 1991

★ Stroke of the Brush I 5.11c/d

Fifty feet right of Vincent's Ear is a left-arching overhanging wall. A lone bolt marks the start.

1. Climb past the bolt (crux) up to a rail, climbing it past two fixed pins and a bolt at the top. 40'

FA: Jon Sykes and Jamie Cunningham July 29, 1996

Echo Crag

This recently developed one-pitch cliff band offers a surprising diversity of excellent crack and face climbs all tucked away in the woods in a beautiful setting. There are also many moderate routes here. With a five- to ten-minute approach to the various parts of the cliff, good views of Cannon Mountain, Echo Lake and the Green Mountains of Vermont, who could ask for more?

There are several relatively distinct sections or walls found along this long cliff band. From left to right they are: The Bouldering Wall, Square Inch Wall, The Shield, Grunge Wall, Poker Pile, Maggot Buttress, Hermit Haven, Hone Wall, and Dream Wall.

If you are coming from the south, follow Route 93 north through Franconia Notch on the Franconia Notch Parkway, and take Parkway Exit 3 (Route 18) for Echo Lake Beach and Peabody Lodge. Take this same exit if you are heading south on Route 93. Park at the Gov. Gallen Memorial itself or at the Echo Lake Beach lot. DO NOT park along the curve, and DO NOT block the road, or you will be ticketed. The approach trail starts right at the curve in the road beside the off ramp from Route 93, ten feet

Looking down on Franconia Notch from Artist's Bluff with the beginning of Echo Crag in the background.   Jamie Cunningham

to the right of a road sign for the viewing area and the Gov. Gallen Memorial. Hike in for several minutes along an easy trail to the cliff base.

The routes at Echo Crag are described from left to right (north to south) as they are encountered when hiking along the base.

The Bouldering Wall

The first climbing you will come to, at the far left-hand end of the cliff, is a twenty-foot high bouldering wall with several good problems. The wall is about sixty feet long, with a three-foot wide arch that curves right across the right hand side.

The Square Inch Wall

The main cliff of Echo Crag boasts a high concentration of routes, mostly because nearly every square inch of the cliff can be climbed. Hike up some stone steps to reach the first routes.

★ Gary's I 5.6 R

An obvious, attractive face climb, and the farthest left-hand route on Square Inch Wall.
1. Climb up a short, pretty, gray face with a lot of horizontal edges.
    40', 5.6 R
FA: Chris Marks and Alan Pilgrim Autumn, 1992

Wrecked Him I 5.7

Begin just to the right of Gary's.
1. Climb up an obvious, right-facing corner to a small, square roof eighteen feet up. Turn the roof on the right, and finish up a crack.
40', 5.7
FA: Pete Kulbacki and Pete Henden August, 1994

Barking Up The Wrong Tree I 5.6

Start ten feet to the right of Wrecked Him. Look for a small, jutting block twelve feet up! Just to the left of Triple Chin, climb straight up blocky ground to a vertical crack. 40', 5.6
FA: Pete Henden, Alan Pilgrim, and Pete Kulbacki July 30, 1995

Triple Chin I 5.8

Start just to the right of Barking Up the Wrong Tree.
1. Face climb straight up through three small ceilings, then up a smooth

face to the top. 40', 5.8

FA: Chris Marks and Alan Pilgrim Summer, 1993

★ Chin-Up I 5.7

Begin five feet right of Triple Chin.

1. Climb up to a stance on top of the triple block, then continue up either a shallow, left-facing corner, or the face just to the right. Finish straight up. 45', 5.7

FA: Chris Marks, Alan Pilgrim, and Pete Henden July, 1993

★ California Potato Chip I 5.8

Start five feet to the right of Chin-Up, at the base of a right-facing, inside corner.

1. Climb up the corner, over an overlap, and head straight up a vertical crack to the top. 45', 5.8

FA: Pete Kulbacki, Alan Pilgrim, and Pete Henden July 23, 1995

★ Widowmaker I 5.6

Start eight feet to the right of the California Potato Chip corner, at a small, wedged block below the left end of some mossy bulges.

1. Climb past the wedged block to a stance, then continue straight up a steep wall on incredibly good horizontal edges and incut buckets. 45', 5.6

FA: Alan Pilgrim, Pete Kulbacki, and Pete Henden July 23, 1995

★ Fast Snatch I 5.8

Start at the same small wedged block as for Widowmaker.

1. Climb past the wedged block to a stance ten feet up, step right, and finish up a shallow finger crack past ledges. 45', 5.8

FA: Pete Henden, Chris Marks, and Alan Pilgrim September 2, 1992

★ Finger Locking Good I 5.9+

Start eight feet right of Fast Snatch.

1. Pull up on suspect flake through an overlap to a steep wall above. Belay at Amnesia anchor. 45', 5.9+

FA: Jon Sykes and Lois LaRock August 6, 1995

Gareth Slattery
pulls down on
the Square
Inch Wall

Jamie Cunningham

★ Mack Jam I 5.9+

1. Start four feet to the right of Finger Locking Good at a hand crack. Finish
on same face above. 45', 5.9+

FA: Pete Henden and Pete Kulbacki July, 1995

Amnesia I 5.8

Start 15 feet to the right of Fast Snatch. A little decomposed at the start.

1. Climb up a shallow, awkward groove (5.8), laybacking over a crumbly bulge. Step right to a shallow finger crack which leads up to a five-foot tall, flaring, right-facing corner. 50', 5.8

FA: Chris Marks and Pete Kulbacki Summer, 1993

★ Ether Madness I 5.8

Start 30 feet to the left of the first wooden ladder, just left of a white ledge at the cliff base.

1. Layback flakes over the initial bulge (5.8), climb a slab to a stance on a horizontal ledge, and finish just to the right of center up a 15-foot high, steep, white wall at a thin, vertical crack. Good but hidden hand holds lead to a huge bucket. 50', 5.8

FA: Chris Marks and Pete Kulbacki August 19, 1992

★ Zoomer I 5.8

Begin 20 feet to the left of the ladder, at the left end of a white ledge.

1. Beginning off the left end of a white ledge, climb up a bulging groove which merges with the shallow, vertical finger crack (5.8) above. Belay at the pine tree/sling anchor. 50', 5.8

FA: Alan Pilgrim and Pete Kulbacki July, 1993

★ Horn of Plenty I 5.7

Start fifteen feet to the left of the first ladder, at the left end of the same white ledge.

1. Climb directly over the left side of the overlap (or just left) past horizontal ledges to the horn, then up the right-hand of two shallow, vertical finger cracks to a large spruce tree. 50', 5.7

FA: Pete Henden and Alan Pilgrim July, 1993

Variation: Why? I 5.10d R

1a. Undercling out the center of the overlap, pull over and climb to the top. 50', 5.10d R

FA: Jon Sykes, Rope-solo May, 1993

★ Rocket I 5.6

Start at the top of the first wooden ladder, at the right-hand end of the overlap.

1. Climb up a short crack/slot, face climb around the right side of the small ledge above, then face climb directly to the top. 60', 5.6

FA: Alan Pilgrim and John Wolfenburger July, 1993

★ Avalanche I 5.7

Begin just to the left of the yellow birch tree at the top of the first wooden ladder.

1. Climb up twin finger cracks (5.7) to a stance, then face climb straight up on buckets to a large pine tree. 60', 5.7

FA: Chris Marks and Alan Pilgrim June, 1993

★ Maiming of the Shrew I 5.5

Start at the yellow birch tree.

1. Climb up the gully directly behind the birch, then climb a right-facing corner on the left to a two-bolt anchor on top. 55', 5.5

FA: Alan Pilgrim, Jamie Cunningham, and Pete Henden June 18, 1995

Variation: Just Kidding I 5.6

1a. At a small overlap halfway up the right-facing corner, step left onto the face, and climb up a clean arete with a shallow, vertical crack. 55', 5.6

FA: Alan Pilgrim, Mark Driscoll, and Pete Henden July 23, 1995

Threading the Alpine Needle I 5.6

Once again, start at the large yellow birch tree.

1. Climb up the easy gully, and follow a wide crack to a ledge and an alcove with a white birch tree. Above, finish up a crack through the center of the top overlap. 60', 5.6

History: Jon Sykes rope-soloed the climb in the winter of 1994. Alan Pilgrim and Pete Kulbacki cleaned the route June 22, 1995, opening up other beautiful climbs in this gully.

★ Piss of Fear I 5.10a

Ten feet to the right of the first wooden ladder are three very large blocks stacked on top of each other.

1. Face-climb up the center of the blocks past two horizontal cracks to the final, committing face move (5.10a) to reach the top of the third block. Above the ledge, continue straight up to a stance, undercling right around an overlap, and climb a short white face to the top. 60', 5.10a

FA: Jamie Cunningham, Ed Webster, and Jon Sykes June 19, 1995

Climber top-roping
Skeletal Ribs

Jon Sykes

★ Skeletal Ribs I 5.6

This is the obvious vertical crack system fifteen feet to the right of the yellow birch.

1. Climb up the slowly widening crack to several ribs of granite on the right, then follow a thin crack over a white bulge to the top. 60', 5.6

FA: Neal Brodien and Jamie Cunningham August, 1992

Anna's Treat I 5.11d

This is the very blank face just to the right of Skeletal Ribs.

1. Bouldering moves lead you up past horizontal cracks; then make desperate face moves (bolt) past a shallow horizontal crack to a stance. Easier climbing leads to the top. 60', 5.11d

History: Jon Sykes placed the bolt free on the lead on June 19, 1995 Finally, in June 2000, Jon Sykes and Eric Pospesil freed the entire route.

Scottish Gully I 5.6
The mossy, usually wet wide crack system just to the right of Anna's Treat. Best climbed in the winter as a moderate mixed route.
1. Climb up the crack to a horizontal break at half height and finish up twin cracks. 60', 5.6
FA: Jamie Cunningham and Neal Brodien August, 1992

Just to the right of the The Scottish Gully are two difficult, bolt-protected face climbs:

Troll Bandit I 5.11d/5.12a
This is the left-hand, bolted route, mossy and often wet.
1. Face climb past two horizontal cracks to a blank face, then steal your way up the smooth face past two bolts to the horizontal break. Above, continue up a white face, and over the center of a small roof. 60'
History: Jon Sykes bolted the route on the lead, placing the first bolt free, and the second on aid in June of 1995.
FFA: Pat Hackett Summer, 1997

★ Cinch Sack I 5.11b
The right-hand, easier, bolted route. The second bolt is very tough to clip.
1. Step up to the two horizontal cracks, then climb a deceivingly difficult 5.11b face past two bolts to the horizontal break. Don't use the outside corner on the right! Continue straight up over small overlaps, with one last hard 5.10 move past the top overlap. 60', 5.11b
FA: Chris Marks and Pete Kulbacki August, 1994

Variation: No Sack I 5.8
1a. Climb up to the first bolt on Cinch Sack, step right, and follow a rounded, vertical finger crack on the outside corner up to the horizontal break. 30', 5.8
History: Alan Pilgrim followed the first ascent of Cinch Sack using this variation in August of 1994.

Eric Carpenter
just moments
before falling off
Cinch Sack

Jamie Cunningham

Sackless   I 5.8

Climb corner (right-facing) to rounded, vertical finger crack and go straight
to top following vertical crack system.
FA: Jon Sykes, rope-solo September, 1994

★ Live Free or Die - Part 2   I 5.11a

It's your choice. A bold climb directly above the second wooden ladder.
1. Face climb up past a bolt to the center of a horizontal overlap, and clip

the bolt just above the lip. Pull over the overlap (5.11a), and head straight up, using a shallow V-crack, directly up to a pine tree. 60', 5.11a
FA: Ken Reville and Jamie Cunningham August, 1992

★ Bee Line I 5.6

Start five feet to the right of the second wooden ladder.
1. Jam up the nice-looking, vertical crack to the top. 60', 5.6
FA: Jamie Cunningham and Neal Brodien August, 1992

No Bolts Please I 5.7

Begin ten feet to the right of Bee Line.
1. Step up to a horizontal crack, then face climb past thin flakes to the horizontal break and a good ledge. Move left to the back of an alcove, then climb up and out to the right before heading straight to the top. 60', 5.7
FA: Jon Sykes and Jamie Cunningham June, 1994

★ VH-1 I 5.7

A classic jam crack at Echo. Start twenty feet to the right of Bee Line.
1. Jam up a ten-foot finger crack (5.7) to the horizontal break, step right, and follow the next finger crack past the left-hand side of a large alcove to a two-bolt belay/rappel anchor on top. 60', 5.7
FA: Chris Marks, Pete Henden, Alan Pilgrim, and Pete Kulbacki August, 1992

Fletch Wilson demonstrates textbook hand-jamming on VH1

Jamie Cunningham

★ Queen Weetamoo I 5.8

Cat-like finesse required. Start a few feet to the right of VH-1.

1. Make bouldering moves (5.8) up the smooth face just to the right of VH-1 to reach the horizontal break. Then climb the next finger crack for ten feet to the left side of the alcove, finishing up and around the left side of the alcove roof (5.6), then climb a fist crack to reach the two-bolt belay/rappel anchor on top. 60', 5.8

History: Pete Henden and Alan Pilgrim made the first ascent on August 13, 1992, naming the route for Henden's cat.

Mean Clean Climb I 5.10d

Real mean if you fall off the roof on the lead! Considerably safer, and much more popular, on a top-rope.

1. Boulder up the vertical seam (5.9) four feet left of Cooler Sacrifice to the horizontal break, and step up to the alcove. After protecting in the tricky flake underneath the roof, crank out the center of the alcove roof (5.10d), continuing up the smooth face five feet left of the pine-tree rappel anchor to the top. 60', 5.10d

FA: Jon Sykes and Jamie Cunningham July, 1994

Three Belches I 5.10b

Climb the start of Cooler Sacrifice to alcove. At the back of the alcove, layback up a vertical crack in a smooth flare (5.10b) up to the pine tree anchor on the left. 60', 5.10b

FA: Chris Marks, Pete Kulbacki, and Pete Henden August 26, 1992

★ Cooler Sacrifice I 5.7

One of the cliff's most popular routes ascends the perfect twin finger cracks up to the alcove at the right-hand end of the Square Inch Wall, sixty feet to the right of the second wooden ladder. Well protected, fun climbing.

1. Climb the twin cracks (5.7) for twenty-five feet to the alcove, then layback an obvious vertical flake (5.6) to the pine tree anchor just overhead. 60', 5.7

History: While cleaning the alcove of ferns and foliage, in their zealousness, Pete Kulbacki, Babben Kulbacki, and Alan Pilgrim accidentally scored a direct hit on their beer cooler with a large rock. They also buried the rest of their gear below with the debris, but nonetheless made the first ascent of this popular line on August 2, 1992. Most important, the beer was saved!

★ Mandrill I 5.9

The sinker, vertical finger crack five feet to the right of Cooler Sacrifice.
1. Jam the initial finger crack (5.9) to gain the right side of the alcove. Continue up to a small overlap (pin) then make a strenuous move past one final, rounded overlap (5.9) to a peg and bolt anchor on top. 60', 5.9
FA: Chris Marks, Alan Pilgrim, Pete Kulbacki, and Pete Henden July 17, 1992

The Shield

This next section of the cliff offers a completely different type of climbing complete with intricate face moves and a series of unlikely, but climbable overlaps. The routes are better than they may appear from below.

Chimbley I 5.4

The shallow, chimney crack five feet to the right of Mandrill.
1. Climb up the shallow chimney to the trees above. 50', 5.4
FA: Pete Kulbacki, Free solo August 1992

Gareth Slattery climbing the Shield   Mike Lee

[Unnamed] I 5.10b

Start three feet to the right of Pappy's Pearl.

1. Climb up a clean white face to a horizontal break then up past horizontal cracks to the center ledge. Cross over the previous route to its left and swing out the center of a blocky overhang (5.10b) past two bolts. 80', 5.10b

History: The lower 5.9 face was first climbed by Jon Sykes and Jamie Cunningham in July 1993, leading to Pappy's Pearl.

The first ascent of the upper bolted overhang is unknown.

★ Pappy's Pearl I 5.10a

Start 20 feet to the right of Mandrill.

1. Climb a finger crack into a short chimney, up to the center ledge, then crank out the blocky overhang via a vertical finger crack (5.10a) to jugs at the lip. 70', 5.10a

FA: Chris Marks and Pete Kulbacki September, 1992

★ Ed's Weed-Be-Gone I 5.10b

Here one day, gone the next! One of Echo's best roof problems.

1. Jam up the vertical crack (5.5) just to the right of Unnamed to the center ledge. Next climb up several stacked blocks past one birch tree until you are beneath the upper roof. Move up to the roof (bolt), reach a jug on the left of the lip, and crank up to a horizontal crack above. 80', 5.10b

History: Jon Sykes rope-soloed the first ascent, placed the crux bolt on aid, returned an hour later with Bill Howe, and made the first free ascent, all on August 1, 1995.

★ Wesley's Aspirations I 5.10d

Start thirty-five feet to the right of Mandrill.

1. Climb up a cleaned face to a stance on the horizontal break. Continue up the face past more horizontal cracks with a 5.9 balance/slab move up to a ledge at half height. Step up to the left-hand end of a small arch (bolt) just below the top of the cliff. Pull past the arch to a second bolt (5.10d) and go for the top. 80', 5.10d

History: Jamie Cunningham, Jon Sykes, and Chris Marks made the ascent on June 17, 1993, naming the route for Jamie's son, Wesley.

Blueberry Wanna Be I 5.9+

1. Climb dirty corner five feet right of Wesley's to ledges above, clip bolt (hard) on Damn It, Jon! and climb to the top.

FA: Jon Sykes and Gareth Slattery August, 1995

Damn It, Jon! I 5.9+ R

Start 20 feet to the right of Wesley's Aspirations below a narrow, cleaned face just to the left of a dirty toe of rock. Modern rack and tricky protection.

1. Climb the left edge of the cleaned face past a small, easy overlap. Continue up a short face (5.9+ crux) with a V-crack to the center ledge. Climb through the middle of a series of larger overlaps (5.9) to the final face (bolt, 5.8). 80', 5.9+ R

FA: Jamie Cunningham and Jon Sykes June 17, 1993

Jesus, Jim! I 5.9+ R

Begin just to the right of Damn It, Jon!

1. Face climb up the initial face to a stance on a three-foot tall, right-facing corner. Puzzle up the face above (5.9+) to a ledge. Then climb a big, left-facing flake and swing past two more overlaps (beware of flakes) to more tricky moves just below the top. 80', 5.9+ R

FA: Jon Sykes and Jamie Cunningham June 17, 1993

Not Lichen It I 5.9+ R

1. Climb thin face between Jesus, Jim! and Lichen It to a very large, hollow flake (danger). Climb face of flake to a left-facing corner, out this to the top.

FA: Jon Sykes, Sean Slattery, Gareth Slattery, and Jamie Cunningham Summer, 1993

★ Lichen It I 5.8

Start 10 feet right of Jesus, Jim! at the left side of the dark toe of rock.

1. Climb up a groove for 20 feet then move up and right to a right-facing flake. Continue over a bulge to the bulge above and finish up a nice, short finger crack. 70'

FA: Jon Sykes and Jamie Cunningham September, 1992

★ Crucial Evidence I 5.9+

Ten feet to the right of Lichen It, belay on a small stance above the toe of rock. The start of the route is identified by a bolt on a smooth slab to the left of a small scoop with another bolt just to the right, which is on Social Experiment.

1. Face climb up the slab (bolt, 5.9+), making very thin moves to a horizontal crack. Next climb around the left side of a large overlap, finishing up assorted cracks directly to the top. 60', 5.9+

FA: Jon Sykes, Rope-solo July, 1994

★ Social Experiment I 5.10b

Takes a direct line through the overlaps after a technical slab at the start. Begin 10 feet to the right of Crucial Evidence. Carry a modern rack.

1. Make hard face moves up the slab (5.10b) past the starting bolt to a horizontal crack and a good ledge on the right below the center of the main overlap. Protect, pull up (crux) to the next overlap, and swing through to easier terrain up a steep, fun face to a tree anchor. 60', 5.10b

FA: Jon Sykes and Jamie Cunningham July 21, 1994

Catapult I 5.9+

Scramble up the toe of rock to a ledge below the right-hand end of the main overlap.

1. Climb up and slightly left, directly over the right-hand section of the main overlap (5.9+). Pull around a second, smaller overlap (5.9) at a wedged block, then climb straight up the final face (5.6). 60', 5.9+

FA: Jamie Cunningham and Jon Sykes October, 1992

★ The Shield I 5.7

Start at the right-hand side of the toe of the rock just to the left of a large pine tree and two large white flakes.

1. From a stance on top of the two flakes, move up a 20-foot high buttress to a ledge below an overlap. Now step over the left side of that overlap into a thin, vertical crack splitting the upper face. A final, small overlap leads to the top. 75', 5.7

FA: Jamie Cunningham and Neal Brodien September, 1992

Bow & Arrow I 5.7

Start beside a large pine tree on the right-hand side of the Shield.

1. Climb up a concave wall for 20 feet to the same small ledge as on the Shield. Climb over an overlap to the left of a small bush, step past one more narrow overlap, and climb the face to the top. 75', 5.7

FA: Jamie Cunningham and Lauren Blair July 21, 1995

The Cow's Mouth I 5.5

Start five feet to the right of the large pine tree at the base of the Shield.

1. Climb stepped holds up the dirty buttress to a ledge 25 feet up. Climb a clean, grey face to the next ledge, step over the center of a narrow overlap, and climb to the top. 75', 5.5

FA: Jamie Cunningham and Steve Saffo August 22, 1993

The Grunge Wall

The dirty face to the right of the Shield has two excellent climbs. Sleep in the Dry Spot, the clean, grey stripe of rock up the wall's right-hand side, and Carpet Path.

Rope Snot I 5.6 R

Start at a large, split, white birch tree on the trail at the left end of the wall. It needs cleaning—like its neighbors.

1. Face climb up through the center of a small overlap (the only overlap at the base of this section of the wall) straight to the top. 70', 5.6 R

FA: Jon Sykes, Rope-solo July, 1993

★ Carpet Path I 5.5

A hidden gem that is great for teaching.

1. Face climb straight up, taking a line eight feet to the right of the overlap on Rope Snot. 70', 5.6

FA: Jon Sykes, Rope-solo July, 1993

Just Left I 5.6

Climb the face ten feet to the right of Carpet Path.

1. Climb up a stepped, left-facing corner five feet tall, then face climb up and slightly right to a small corner at the left-hand side of the small, top overlap. Step over the overlap on the left and climb to the top. 70', 5.6

FA: Dave Goodwin and Kris Pastoria July, 1993

Awake in the Wet Spot I 5.7 R

Start 10 feet to the right of the previous route.

1. Climb directly up the lichen-covered face and black streak. 70', 5.7 R

FA: Jon Sykes, Rope-solo July, 1993

★ Sleep in the Dry Spot I 5.6

A classic face route ascending the obvious, clean streak up the Grunge Wall's right-hand side. (Enjoyable moves and reasonable protection.) Carry wired nuts and small cams. Start at a large, white birch tree.

1. Face climb straight up the clean streak on good holds to a tree anchor at the top. 75', 5.6

FA: Alan Pilgrim, Chris Marks, and Pete Henden June 20, 1993

Alpine Grunge I 5.7 R

Begin 10 feet to the right of Sleep in the Dry Spot.

1. Climb a small, very dirty rock rib; head straight to the top. 60', 5.7 R

FA: Jon Sykes and Chris Marks January, 1995

Wesley Cunningham follows in his father's footsteps on the best 5.6 at Echo—Sleep In The Dry Spot

Jamie Cunningham

The Poker Pile

Follow the trail 50 feet to the right from Sleep in the Dry Spot and you will reach a small broken buttress. Access the following routes via stepped ledges on the Pile's left side. Care needed!

Drag Queen I 5.8

Climbs a V-groove up the left side of Poker Pile.
1. Climb up the V-groove into a short chimney, wedge upwards, and step left to a steep face. Make a thin move to the trees. 50', 5.8
FA: Chris Marks and Jon Sykes Spring, 1995

★ Stacked Deck I 5.10b (or 5.11b) 5.8 R

Start below the block, just to the left of the Insider's Strait chimney.
1. Climb the block's arete (pin), then make 5.8 R moves to a second peg and the top of the blocks. Continue up under the main roof, hand traverse right to the lip, and pull over. It's 5.10b if you stem over to the other wall, 5.11b if you don't. 40'
FA: Jon Sykes, Rope-solo July, 1994

Insider's Strait I 5.6

1. Climb the chimney/corner just to the right of Stacked Deck to the trees. 40', 5.6
FA: Jon Sykes, Rope-solo July, 1994

Maggot Buttress

This buttress is just before Hermit Haven. One decent climb can be found here.

★ Lord of the Flies I 5.8

Look for a lone bolt on the smooth face ten feet up.
1. Climb past the bolt (crux) and ascend cracks above to the top. 60', 5.8
FA: Eric Carpenter Spring, 1999

The Hermit Haven

About 100 feet to the right of the Poker Pile, look uphill and you will see The Hermit Haven. If you hike straight ahead, the traversing trail leads to the base of The Hone Wall.

Hermit Power I 5.9

1. Climb the arete and face past pins and bolts just left of Old Route. Beware of loose rock near the top. 60', 5.9

FA: Jon Sykes, Rope-solo Summer, 1999

Old Route I 5.7 Note: Loose rock

1. Climb the obvious, bush-filled dihedrals up the left-hand side of the cliff. 60', 5.7

History: An old gold line rope and steel descending rings were found anchored to a tree at the top of the route. The first ascent is unknown.

★ Hermit Bar I 5.10c

Note: This route has tricky protection and needs cleaning. Start several feet to the left of Hermit Bar and a Motrin.

1. Face climb up the left center of a brown overlap 15 feet above the ground then swing past the overlap (5.10c) to a ledge. Climb the right-facing corner (5.10a) above to a stance, then face climb straight up (bolt) finishing up and right to the top. 60', 5.10c

FA: Jon Sykes and Jamie Cunningham July, 1994

★ Hermit Bar and a Motrin I 5.10b

Gymnastic moves and wild positions! Do yourself a favor: eat, and more importantly, take the Motrin first. Start below the right-hand end of the brown overlap 15 feet off the ground at the center of the face. Normal rack.

1. Climb up a very thin face until under the overlap and mantle (bolt) onto a small stance on the left. Step right then climb shallow corners past two bolts to a partial rest before underclinging right (awkward) until you can position yourself beneath the final, large overlap. Clip a hidden bolt over the lip then pull over with all your remaining strength, if you have any left. A short face gains the top. 70', 5.10b

FA: Jon Sykes, Rope-solo July, 1994
FFA: Jon Sykes and Jamie Cunningham July, 1994

The Hone Wall

This imposing vertical wall is home to nearly all of Echo Crag's sport routes, which in all instances are not really sport routes because they utilize the mere minimum of bolts. Be well advised to bring a modern rack to supplement the existing bolts! You'll be sorry if you go up on one of these routes with only quick draws. RPs, small cams, and Lowe Balls are all helpful. At the far left-hand side of the cliff, a small spring issues forth from the base of the cliff.

Spring Line I 5.7

The left-hand most route up the Hone Wall begins just to the left of the natural spring at the cliff's base. Modern rack.

1. Face climb up the left side of the wall 10′ to the left of Fiddling Jim, finishing over the left-hand overlap (5.7) at the top. 80′, 5.7

FA: Jamie Cunningham, Rope-solo June 8, 1995

Center Line I 5.7 R

Modern rack, including small wired nuts. Start just above the spring.

1. Climb straight up the face five feet to the left of Fiddling Jim, finishing

The Hone Wall (left) and Dreamwall (right)   Jamie Cunningham

up the face between the two top overlaps. 80', 5.7 R
FA: Jamie Cunningham and Eric Klieber July 6, 1995

★ Fiddling Jim I 5.6

Start 100 feet to the right of the Hermit Wall and five feet right of the natural spring. Bring a modern rack.
1. Climb to a ledge 15 feet up, then face climb straight up a clean, grey face, finishing over the right-hand overlap at the top. 80', 5.6
FA: Jamie Cunningham and Jon Sykes July 20, 1994

The Hone Wall - Upper Tier

This somewhat hidden cliff band is directly above Fiddling Jim. The access ledges to reach the Upper Tier are located 10 feet left of Blueberry Knoll. Scramble up the ledges (5.0) to reach a two-bolt belay/rappel anchor at the base of the Upper Tier. Routes are described from left to right.

★ Berlin Girls Buck Back I 5.7

1. Climb a finger crack (5.7) up the short, white headwall located up and left of the two-bolt anchor. 40', 5.7
FA: Pete Kulbacki, Babben Kulbacki, and Alan Pilgrim; September, 1993

Don't Stink In My House I 5.4

Another Berlin (New Hampshire) tradition. Ascends the short, broken vertical groove directly above the two-bolt anchor.
1. Above a white birch, climb up a broken groove. 40', 5.4
FA: Alan Pilgrim, Babben Kulbacki, and Pete Kulbacki September, 1993

Wait, Too Late I 5.6

This route is to the right of the two-bolt belay. Start 10 feet to the right of Berlin Girls Buck Back.
1. Climb a steep, white headwall, finishing on good holds. 40' 5.6
FA: Jon Sykes, Rope-solo September, 1993

The following climbs all are located on the main section of The Hone Wall.

Blueberry Knoll I 5.7 R

Climb the first clean face five feet to the right of the Upper Tier access ledges and 30 feet to the left of Bits & Pieces.

---

1. Climb up a clean face to a birch tree belay. Hard mantle move near the top. 50', 5.7 R

FA: Jamie Cunningham and Eric Klieber July 6, 1995

Bits and Pieces I 5.9

Start 30 feet to the right of Blueberry Knoll, just left of a left-facing corner.

1. Climb up a face to the left of a left-facing corner to a steep wall, then climb alpine terrain to the trees. 80', 5.9

FA: Jon Sykes, Rope-solo August, 1994

Spunky Pig I 5.10a (5.9 R)

Start 10 feet right of Bits & Pieces (15 feet left of NCO Take-Off) at the left-hand end of The Hone Wall. Modern rack.

1. Climb straight up a clean face (5.9 R) to a horizontal ledge, then face climb past one bolt (5.10a) to the top. 80', 5.10a (5.9 R)

History: Jamie Cunningham and Jon Sykes made the first ascent on September 12, 1993, placing the bolt free on the lead.

NCO Take-Off I 5.10d (left) or 5.10b (right)

Steep face climbing with mostly natural protection that is tricky to place. Begin five feet to the left of the rectangular block on No Pigs.

1. Move up fractured rock (pin) and face climb straight up the upper face past two bolts to the top. If you go left of the second bolt it is 5.10d; moving right of the bolt is 5.10b. 80', 5.10d or 5.10b

History: Jon Sykes and Jamie Cunningham made the first ascent on September 12, 1993, placing the bolts on the lead.

★ No Pigs I 5.8

One of Echo's best routes, but widely-spaced bolt protection ensures that only the fittest will survive. A 5.8 face climb for 5.10 leaders. Start at the center/left side of the main Hone Wall below a rectangular block 10 feet up. The first bolt is 20 feet up, under the left end of a narrow overlap. Carry a small normal rack.

1. Above the block, face climb up and left past two bolts. Move slightly left, step back right (5.8), clip the third bolt (with relief), then make hard, balancy face moves (5.8) to the final bolt. Easier climbing gains the top and a two-bolt belay/rappel anchor. 90', 5.8

History: Jamie Cunningham and Ken Reville made the first ascent in August, 1992, after placing the bolts on rappel.

The author leads the classic No Pigs on the Hone Wall

Jamie Cunningham

Hexmate I 5.10b R

Takes a bold line up the very steep face just to the right of No Pigs. Modern rack, definitely!

1. After clipping the first bolt on No Pigs, step right and face climb straight up (5.10b R) to a lonely bolt step right into a groove, then back left on to the upper face (5.9 R) which is climbed to a two-bolt belay/rappel anchor. 90', 5.10b R

History: Ken Reville and Jamie Cunningham made the first ascent in August, 1992, placing the crux bolt on the lead.

Broken Dreams I 5.9 R

Start to the far right by Just Roof'n Around.

1. Follow a ledge system diagonally up and left to a right-facing, flaring corner in the upper center of the wall. 90', 5.9 R

History: Unknown. An old sling was found around a tree at the top.

★ Race Day I 5.9+

This route was first bolted on rappel on July 26, 1993, by Jon Sykes and Jamie Cunningham in a race with the other team of first ascentists at Echo. A few years later Jon removed the bolts, disappointed by his actions in 1993. In the summer of 2000, Jon re-established the route rope-solo, placing all the bolts on lead.

1. Five feet to the right of Broken Dreams, a line of widely-spaced bolts leads up a steep face. Follow these bolts past a small overlap to a two-bolt belay. Bring a small rack.

FA: Jon Sykes, Rope-solo Summer, 2000

★ Rain Dance I 5.9+

Start fifteen feet to the right of Broken Dreams, and Ten feet left of Just Roof'n Around. Modern rack.

1. Climb over the first overlap past two bolts (5.9+) on large holds, then dance up the upper face past two more bolts, making more strenuous 5.9+ moves to the top. 90', 5.9+

★ Just Roof'n Around I 5.11b

Another Hone Wall classic. Look for two bolts protecting an overlap/roof 20 feet up on the right-hand section of the Hone Wall's main face. V-Chimney is directly overhead, at the top of the cliff.

1. Climb on moderate ground up to the overlap/roof, which is well protected by two bolts. Sequential moves (5.11b) lead out the roof onto the upper face which has two more bolts and excellent holds (5.9+). Belay at a two-bolt fixed anchor at the top. 90', 5.11b

FA: Jon Sykes and Jamie Cunningham, July 17, 1993

V-Chimney I 5.8 R

Climb the V-chimney high up on the right side of the main Hone Wall. Begin 10 feet right of Just Roof'n Around, 10 feet left of a pine tree. Beware of loose rock.

Claudine Safar cranks down on Just Roofin' Around   Jamie Cunningham

1. Follow bushy ledges up and left to gain the final V-chimney (5.8 R) at the top. 90', 5.8 R

History: The first ascent is unknown. An old piton was found.

God I Love This! I 5.9+

This hidden gem offers great alpine climbing. Begin ten feet to the right of Just Roof'n Around.

1. Climb blocky ground with ledges and loose rock then traverse five feet right (pin) across a ledge. Face climb (bolt, 5.9+) up the face just left of Hurry Up I'm Hungry's second overlap, then left, finishing up a smooth face (pin) to a two-bolt belay. 90', 5.9+

FA: Jon Sykes, Rope-solo June, 1994

★ Hurry Up, I'm Hungry I 5.10d or 5.10b

Begin on the right-hand side of The Hone Wall below and 10 feet left of a large prominent pine tree growing 30 feet up the cliff. The route has two obvious overlaps: 5.10d moving left at the overlap, or 5.10b, moving right.

1. Climb a short, steep face (bolt) to the pine tree, then face climb up (bolt) and left to the first overlap (bolt) before moving up to the next, bigger overlap. Climb through the middle of this overlap (bolt, 5.10d), then

cruise straight up the face to a platform. Finish up and left. 90', 5.10d (or, as noted above 5.10b)

History: Jamie Cunningham and Jon Sykes attempted the route and placed the third bolt in July of 1993. Jon Sykes returned in June of 1994 and rope-soloed the first complete ascent, placing the upper bolt from sky-hooks.

Sling'n The Pitch I 5.9

Start directly below the large pine tree. Normal rack needed; no bolts!

1. Head up to the tree, then climb the face directly behind the pine, straight up over a small overlap directly to the top. 90', 5.9

FA: Jon Sykes and Jamie Cunningham August 28, 1993

★ Pig's Knuckles I 5.9+

Start below the obvious large pine tree.

1. Face climb straight up, five feet to the right of the pine tree past the two bolts. Move over an overlap, then trend up and right, up cracks to the final bulge. 90', 5.9+

FA: Jamie Cunningham and Jon Sykes July 27, 1993

★ The Big Tweak I 5.10c

(5.10c if you climb above the bolt, 5.11a if you move right at the bolt.)

1. Face climb up to the first bolt on Lycra, then step left, and move up to a stance (bolt). Face climb past a flake and overlap to a ledge below the left side of the large overhang above. Make tweaky face moves right (bolt) out the overhang, and onto the upper slab. 90', 5.10c or 5.11a

FA: Jon Sykes and Jamie Cunningham October 1, 1993

★ Ants in Your Lycra I 5.10a

Highly recommended! Locate a beautiful, clean, grey face capped by a long roof or overlap at the far, right end of The Hone Wall, twenty-five feet to the right of a large pine tree. Normal rack.

1. Face climb up the center of a grey face past the first bolt to a good stance. Make 5.8 moves up and right to better holds, then angle up right to a two-bolt belay/rappel anchor at a short, left-facing corner splitting the right side of the roof. Stop here (at 5.8) and rappel off, or clip the anchor and pull past the roof on the right (5.10a, bolt) to a pine tree anchor at the top. 90', 5.10a

FA: Chris Marks and Alan Pilgrim July, 1993

★ Forty Ways to Stay Young I 5.10c

The face just to the right of Ants in Your Lycra. Normal rack.

1. Face climb up the grey face (5.10a) immediately right of Lycra past two bolts and join Lycra at the two-bolt anchor above. Finish up the crux overhang just left of Lycra (bolt) to a two-bolt belay.

FA: Jon Sykes, Rope-solo July, 1994 (Lower grey face)
FA: Jon Sykes, Eric Carpenter, and Jamie Cunningham August, 1998 (Upper overhang)

Author getting a little loose on the first attempt of Forty Ways To Stay Young

Jamie Cunningham

French Connection I 5.7

Begin thirty feet to the right of Lycra below a small secluded face.

1. Climb up the face to a tree ledge. 35', 5.3

2. Head up a slab to a weakness through the overlap (5.7) that is twenty-five feet to the right of the crux of Lycra. Finish up a slab to a tree belay. 60', 5.7

FA: Alan and Caroline Pilgrim July, 1993

The Dream Wall

The final wall on the cliff has an obvious nose on the left, the line of the Arete, and a prominent overhang on the upper right, Ten Years Later. Both the arete and the roof are visible from the highway.

Twilight I 5.8

Contrived face moves on nice rock up the left side of the arete. Normal rack, with a small TCU.

1. Face climb straight up past four bolts (5.8) to a flake/crack, and finish at the two-bolt belay/rappel anchor at the top of the Arete. 80', 5.8

FA: Alan Pilgrim, Steve Saffo, and Jamie Cunningham August 27, 1993

Variation: North of North I 5.8

1a. Face climb past the second bolt on Twilight (5.8), step off left into the woods, and face climb up the center (5.7) of the left-hand face to the top and a two-bolt anchor. 80', 5.8

FA: Jamie Cunningham, Alan Pilgrim, and Steve Saffo August 27, 1993

★ The Arete I 5.8

The prominent, rounded arete on the left side of the Dream Wall is one of Echo Crag's best routes. Bring wired nuts, small cams. Begin just to the right of the nose.

1. Face climb up clean rock (5.8) to easier moves straight up on excellent holds past horizontal cracks and ledges to a stance (piton). Continue up a shallow, left-facing flake in a steeper wall (5.8) to a moderate face with big holds leading to a two-bolt belay anchor. You can rappel off the anchor with a 165' rope if you tension over toward the woods. 120', 5.8

History: This line was most likely climbed in the 1970s. Chris Marks and Alan Pilgrim placed the two-bolt anchor on July 15, 1992, and found an old piton and sling at half height.

Route With A View I 5.8 (5.7 R)

Start thirty feet to the right of The Arete.

1. Face climb up a cleaned streak of rock (5.5) between two mossy sections to reach the center tree ledge to the right of the mid-section of The Arete. 40', 5.5

2. Face climb up for twenty feet, traverse left across a slab to thin cracks, and climb straight up a short face. Finish over the left side of a roof/overlap (5.8) and up on an orange face (5.7 R) to a two-bolt belay/rappel anchor. 75', 5.8 (5.7 R)

FA: Jon Sykes and Tim Burke Summer, 1993

★ Psychotic Realization I 5.12b

The name says it all. The hardest route at Echo ascends the blank slab and roof just to the right of Route With a View.

1. Climb the first pitch of View, up the clean streak (5.5).

2. Move up a short, steep face to a slab and the first bolt. Climb thin moves (5.9) to a bulge, make a hard clip at the second bolt, then power up desperate face moves (5.12b) on a smooth face until underneath the main roof. Make an awkward move to good holds at the lip. Protect and pull over (5.10a), finishing up a face (5.8) to a two-bolt belay/rappel anchor. 75', 5.12b

FA: Jon Sykes, Rope-solo Spring, 1994
FFA: Jon Sykes with Fletcher Wyman May, 1995

★ Ten Years Later I 5.10b (5.6 R)

Sometimes a good idea is worth remembering! Takes a line up the blank slab to the right of the crux moves of Psychotic Realization.

1. Climb the first pitch of Buck-Toothed Chicken Splitter.

2. Head up a 20-foot steep face (5.6 R) to a lone bolt on a slab. Now make thin moves up a blank wall (5.10a) to a hidden flake/bucket. Move left up a slanting groove to the roof, then over it on the left (5.10b) to a stance. Follow a crack much more easily to the same 2-bolt anchor shared by the preceding routes. 75', 5.10b (5.6 R)

FA: Jon Sykes, Tim Burke, and Jamie Cunningham June 17, 1993. Bolt placed on lead.

★ Buck-Toothed Chicken-Splitter I 5.8

The upper pitch takes a wicked line through the top overhang. Start 40 feet to the right of the Arete.

1. Climb up a rounded buttress with cracks (5.5) to the center tree ledge (slings). 50', 5.5

2. Continue face climbing straight up into a prominent, left-arching thin flake system. Undercling/layback up left until it is possible to step up and right and over the arch (5.8). Move up underneath the huge roof then make awkward 5.7 moves out the horizontal crack heading left to the lip, pulling over on good holds (5.7). Belay on a beautiful ledge at a two-bolt belay/rappel anchor. 80', 5.8

History: One of the first modern routes at the cliff. The first ascent party bushwacked up to the start from the highway. Chris Marks, Alan Pilgrim, and Pete Henden made the first ascent on July 8, 1992.

Nail Ripper I 5.7 C2

The farthest right-hand route on the Dream Wall and at Echo Crag. To the right of Chicken-Splitter is a short, steep headwall.

1. Climb up a 70-foot face via a groove at the right-hand end of the Dream Wall to a tree belay. 70', 5.7

2. Head up and left (5.5) to reach the right side of the big roof visible from the road, then aid a broken crack system (C2) to the top. 70', 5.5, C2

History: Jon Sykes took a 15-foot fall when an RP pulled. The fall resulted in the ripping of Sykes' fingernail, hence the name, Nail Ripper.

FA: Jon Sykes, Rope-solo Spring, 1994

Echo Crag Girdle I 5.8

The left to right girdle traverse of the Square Inch Wall, the Shield, and the Grunge Wall. Starting at the Square Inch Wall, traverse right following the horizontal break. Boulder along the base of the Shield Face and traverse right across the Grunge Wall, finishing up Sleep in the Dry Spot.

FA: Jon Sykes, Free-solo May, 1995

Val Michaud belays her daughter on Skeletal Ribs, Square Inch Wall

John Hession

Hone Wall Girdle II 5.10a

The left to right girdle traverse of The Hone Wall.

1. Start at the left side of the Wall. Traverse right through bushes, along broken ledges, and across a steep, lichen-covered wall to a hanging belay just before the steep, main section of the Wall. 90', 5.8

2. Step down, traverse right, and clip the first bolt on Spunky Pig. Clip the first bolt on NCO Take-Off and clip the first bolt on No Pigs before down climbing (5.8), or traversing straight right and down (5.10), to reach the second bolt on Hexmate. Traverse farther right over Broken Dreams and clip the bolt on Rain Dance. Climb up to the last bolt on Just Roof'n Around. Now traverse right from Just Roof'n Around's second bolt under the V-Chimney. Set up another hanging belay at the top bolt and overlap on Hurry Up, I'm Hungry. 150', 5.9 or 5.10

3. Undercling while traversing right below a small overhanging section, then climb up and right to easy traversing to the two-bolt belay below the crux overhang on Ants in Your Lycra on a good ledge. Climb the 5.10a crux overhang of Ants then traverse right on easy ledges to reach the Dream Wall. Climb up and right and belay at the top of the Dream Wall. 150', 5.10

FA: Jon Sykes and Jamie Cunningham July 21, 1994

Profile Cliff

Resting high above Echo Crag, this proud little dome has a great variety of climbs from 80 to 150 feet long. Sweeping vistas of Vermont to the west and of the Notch to the south make this a wonderful location.

Directions: The trail to Profile Cliff starts on the Echo Crag Trail and branches off left under a large dead spruce tree about 300 feet in. A fifteen to twenty minute hike up the trail brings you to the northern end of Profile. Routes will be described from left to right as you approach the cliff.

Warning: No fires or camping are allowed in this area due to a careless act by young locals who caught underground roots on fire and left trash behind. Let's not let something like this happen again, please.

★ Horny Irishman 5.7 R

This is the first climb on the cliff's left side. Turn left when the trail meets the cliff and you will see a steep, short wall with two climbs on it. Horny Irishman climbs the steep, juggy face on the left side of wall. Rap off of two pins hidden in the trees. 60'
FA: Gareth Slattery and Jon Sykes May 28, 1996

One Move and You're Done 5.9 R

On the right side of the wall one can see a lone bolt 40 feet up on the right of the arete. Climb up to corner (natural pro), then up the arete to a bolt, then step left onto face and climb straight to same belay as Horny Irishman. There is a direct line over the roof left of the arete. 60'
FA: Jon Sykes and Lois LaRock May 27, 1996

★ Talus Chimney 5.6

To the left of Talus Spire is a chimney corner system formed by the spire and the other wall to the left. Climb up between two walls until near the top of the spire and climb the left wall up to a little roof—pull over this to trees. Rap off tree with one rope down a gully. 120'
FA: Chris Rowins and friend 1970s

Bad Air Day 5.9+ R

When the trail meets the cliff you will see Talus Spire and a crumbling crack in a left-facing corner leading through a small roof with loose blocks. Climb through these on thought-provoking gear (crux). Follow corner

1. Horny Irishman 5.7 R
2. One Move and You're Done 5.9 R
3. Bad Air Day 5.9+ R
4. Flexing Flake Fest 5.10d
5. Pit Ripper 5.12a
6. Natural High 5.7
7. Tip's Terror 5.10c
8. Syko's Arete 5.11b
9. Birthday Bolts 5.9
10. Crystal Crack 5.8
11. Crystal Biting Good 5.10a
12. Salomon Says 5.6

Climbing Routes for Profile Cliff

above to top of spire. 80′

FA: Jon Sykes and Gareth Slattery May 3, 1996

★ Flexing Flake Fest 5.10d

Just right of B.A.D. is a huge bulge just off the ground with a bolt 10 feet up. The first free ascent started beside the boulder and climbed a feldspar knob on the face (5.11d). The knob, however, broke before a second ascent was completed. One can start off the boulder and traverse left to the bolt, then up to a pin and climb directly up the face above to the top of the spire. 70′

FA: Jon Sykes and Gareth Slattery April 26, 1996

FFA: Jon Sykes and Gareth Slattery May 28, 1996

Hike up past Talus Spire to the left end of the main wall and an obvious corner with flat stones at the base: this is Natural High.

Poacher 5.9+

Just left of the Natural High corner is a broken stack of rock creating a left-facing crack corner. Climb face to right of corner and protect in crack (15′). The climbing eases above until one comes to an arching left-facing corner. Thin wires at the top of the arch get you around the corner (crux); it's very tricky through here. Alpine climbing above, with the usual loose rock, leads to a belay on top of Poacher Pile. Rap with one rope. 90′

FA: Bill Lowther and Bill Keiler May 15, 1996

★ Pit Ripper 5.12a

Climb directly between Poacher and High X. Look for a bolt 40 feet up on a slightly overhung wall. Climb past this (hard), then up to a pin, stepping past this on the left. Another bolt on a much larger overlap (crux) takes you to the top of Poacher Pile.

FA: Jon Sykes and Eric Pospesil July 17, 1996

FFA: Mike Kenney and Jon Sykes September 27, 1998

History: Off the couch, with very little climbing that summer, Mike Kenney on-sight flashed the first free ascent of Pit Ripper in a brilliant display of athletic control of mind and body. It was a pleasure to watch Mike nail it that day after my own struggles with the route.

★ High-X 5.7

This is a hidden gem in the world of exposure. Climb up same start as

Natural High; at the corner step left out onto the arete (pin) and up under the right end of overhung wall (pin). Step right following good holds with big air below to the top of Poacher Pile. Beware of blocks near the top.
FA: Bill Lowther May 15, 1996

★ Natural High 5.7

Climb inside corner to a left-facing flake; up the flake to a stance sixty feet up. Traverse right eight feet, then make balance moves over a diagonal crack to face and climb white dike system above between two white blocks to flake on left. Climb it on the left of the flake to a two-bolt belay above.
FA: Jon Sykes, Rope-solo April 22, 1996

★ Tempered, Not 5.9

Climb the arete ten feet to the right of Natural High past a lone bolt twenty feet up. Go past the bolt on steep face to the diagonal crack, climbing the face directly above to a right-facing corner (pin). Climb to the top of corner then step left and up to cracks above little overlap, climbing cracks and face to top. 150'
FA: Jon Sykes and Lois LaRock April 28, 1996

★ Numb from the Waist Down 5.10a

Boulder up to first bolt (twenty feet), in a shallow, right-facing corner. Next climb up under a roof where a diagonal crack passes by from right to left. Pull through the roof (bolt) to the crux; then steep, pumpy face climbing leads to a large horizontal crack system. Step left five feet to white dike on Natural High, climbing it then going straight up through face climbing to belay on Natural High. 150'
FA: Jon Sykes and Gareth Slattery May 7, 1996

★ Tip's Terror 5.10c

Twenty feet right of Numb from the Waist Down is a striking seam shooting up a steep wall. Climb through a diagonal crack to bolt and face climbing leading to the seam. Follow the seam, face climbing on very steep rock past a second bolt. Continue past this to another bolt and a right-facing corner above (pin). Climb the blocky wall left of corner to one more bolt and tricky face climbing leading to one more small face under a huge block. Climb face trending left around block to belay. 150'
FA: Jon Sykes and Gareth Slattery May 14, 1996

Jamie
Cunningham leads
Natural High

Jon Sykes

★ Love Me Tender 5.8

1. Climb the classic diagonal crack to a natural belay in a corner. Hard climbing in the 5.8 realm.

FA: Bill Keiler, Jon Sykes, and Gareth Slattery May 7, 1996

2. From the belay, climb up corner and right, by-passing most of the loose rock. Then connect with Tempered Not at the overlap, climbing crack and face.

FA: Bill Keiler and Jamie Cunningham May 27, 1996

Ajilla Pospesil
follows
Tempered, Not!

Jon Sykes

★ Syko's Arete 5.11b

A pin marks the start through the overlap. Climb quartz dike above it to a stance. Step left and up to first bolt forty feet off the ground. Now diagonal right on a steep face to second bolt and harder climbing to a third bolt and a hard clip. Pull past this to a fourth bolt and climb up to a steep wall with natural pro above this. Follow along the arete proper past loose blocks to one more face with a huge block on the left. Climb to top and a tree belay on a comfy ledge. Rap with two ropes. 160'

FA: Jon Sykes and Bill Keiler April 25, 1996

★ Beginning of the End 5.7

Just left of Birthday Bolts is a short, right-facing corner. Climb it then step left into the main, right-facing, arching corner. Follow corner up until you meet a block; climb it on the left to a belay station in a corner. 90'
FA: Bill Keiler and Jamie Cunningham May 27, 1996

★ Birthday Bolts 5.9

1. Climb straight up past bolt on steep face to horizontals and flakes. Over this to face climbing past another bolt up to a noticeable break in the wall. Climb through this to a fixed belay in an alcove.
2. Climb corner up through to awkward moves up and left to an arching corner. Climb the arch all the way up and go left at top on a steep face, easier on the right. (The second pitch may have been climbed by Tom Lyman in the 1970s.) 150'
FA: Bill Keiler and Jon Sykes May 15, 1996

★ Chilled to the Bone 5.9 R

One bolt fifteen feet up marks the start. Climb past bolt on steep face trending a little right as you climb to horizontal shallow cracks—marginal cams here (crux). Face-climb past this with better gear until one comes to an arete with a bolt. Head up this to one more steep wall (pin) to your right. Climb over this (loose rock) to a stance and traverse left to fixed belay. Rap with one rope or continue to top. 90'
FA: Jon Sykes and Bill Keiler April 29, 1996

★ SKL Direct 5.8 R

An arm-pumping start directly through the bulge between Chilled to the Bone and Crystal Crack Bulge. Climb through bulge with tricky pro to flake, then past this to horizontal cracks and connect with Crystal Crack face following it to belay in alcove.
FA: Jon Sykes, Bill Keiler, and Bill Lowther May 15, 1996

★ Crystal Crack Bulge 5.9

A direct start to Crystal Crack. Climb up to and left of Crystal Crack and pull over bulge and meet with face above.
FA: Jon Sykes and Lois LaRock May 5, 1996

★ Crystal Crack 5.8

1. Climb face and crack on right side of bulge to face climbing that leads

Ken Reville starts Birthday Bolts   Jamie Cunningham

to another steep face (pin). Continue up this, past loose rock to a stance, and traverse left to fixed belay. 80', 5.8

FA: Jon Sykes and Bill Keiler April 23, 1996

2. From the belay, climb thin flake on left; at top of flake step right ten feet and climb up blocky loose corner, which leads to the top and lookout ledge with a tree belay. 70', 5.8

FA: Jon Sykes, Lois LaRock, and Dawn Pare May 5, 1996

First Route 5.7

First Route starts in corner to the right of Crystal Crack and climbs up a corner for thirty feet, then turns left in another corner, heading up this diagonally left (old hex found in a crack). You're now face-climbing up left past an old pin. Climb over this past loose rock to a stance and belay on left in alcove. The climb then goes around the corner—easy ground but loose rock here. We found two more pins that were rotted in half. No more signs of pins after that. The first part up to the belay is nice, thought-provoking climbing.

FA: Tom Lyman and friend 1970s

★ Crystal Biting Good 5.10a

Climb up corner to the right of Crystal Crack until you come to an arching flake on your right; it's tricky getting onto flake. Layback up flake (sharp) to its top past some small trees and up to a stance under a slightly overhung face with a crack going up it. Climb face and crack to its top (crux) to a tree belay. 110′

FA: Jon Sykes and Lois LaRock April 28, 1996

★ Laybuckin 5.7

Between Crystal Biting Good and Commit to Your Maker is an arching, right-facing corner crack. Climb corner up to another corner; go up this to a slightly overhung face with horizontal jugs. Pull over this to tree belay on left. 100′

FA: Jon Sykes and Sean Slattery June 2, 1996

★ Commit to Your Maker 5.10a

This is the farthest right crack line on the main wall. Five feet right of Old Route corner. Boulder over bulge, then climb easier ground up forty feet of slab until you reach overlap and the crack on a steep wall. Step left and surmount the overlap and traverse along the top of overlap right until you make hard moves getting into the crack. Climb crack to

Ken Reville samples Crystal Crack's second pitch. Cannon Mtn. is in the background.

Jamie Cunningham

another face above with cracks on it; climb juggy face and corner up to tree belay on left. (You can climb directly through the overlap to the crack at 5.10c.) 120'

FA: Jon Sykes, Dawn Pare, and Lois LaRock May 5, 1996

War Drums 5.7

Just right of Commit to Your Maker is a blocky overlap leading to a flake. Climb overlap past flake following cracks up to a bulge. Face climb up the bulge to an overlap with jugs; pull over this to bushes, through these to an upper wall, climbing it on the left up white rock (5.5) to belay. 150'

FA: Jon Sykes and Sean Slattery June 2, 1996

Aztec Warrior 5.7

This is the farthest route on the right side of the main wall. You must bushwhack up to a nice, hidden alcove. Looking at the start of the climb you can see the Aztec warrior head outlined by cracks. Climb corner up fifteen feet, then step right onto face with juggy flakes, and climb this to bushes. Push through the bushes and climb the wall above on right side following a left-facing arch until you can pull through the arch on face holds, leading to a belay. 130'

FA: Jon Sykes and Sean Slattery June 2, 1996

Gareth Slattery tops out on Profile. Notice his sister, Sam, on the
ledge below.   Jon Sykes

Secrets of the Notch • 157

Salomon's Wall

Salomon Says 5.6
On the small wall just past the main cliff on the right, a striking bouldering crack goes up the left of a small wall. Salomon Says starts thirty feet to the right at a quartz dike on a steep face. Climb dike to stance ten feet up, then follow weakness up to the top. Hike off. 60'
FA: Jon Sykes, Solo Summer, 1996

Hike south past Salomon's Wall to the Bad Boy Boulders.
Three climbs can be found here starting from left to right:

★ Speak No More 5.10a
FA: Jon Sykes, Rope-solo July 10, 1996
FFA: Zach Alberts July, 1996

★ Firecracker 5.11b/c
FA: Jon Sykes, Top rope July 4, 1998

★ One Mighty Move 5.11b/c
FA: Jon Sykes, Rope-solo Summer, 1997

Lois LaRock tops out on Natural High in early spring   Jon Sykes

Hound's Hump Ridge

Of all the climbing in Franconia Notch, the least is known of this diverse alpine playground. Some of the area's most rewarding climbs can be found here. The Ridge, which weaves its way along the western flanks of Mt. Lafayette, offers climbers the opportunity to explore remote alpine routes in one of the most dramatic settings in the East. Starting from the north end at Split Rock, it runs south to Resolution Buttress, below and left of Eagle Cliff. There is over a mile's worth of cragging, yet only twenty-five known routes exist due to factors such as long approaches, bushwhacking up steep forested slopes, and of course the alpine climbing with its loose rock and lichen-covered faces. Hidden under these facades are classic crack and face climbs worth the effort hiking there. Routes will be described from left to right (north to south), starting with Split Rock. The importance of self-reliance while in a wilderness setting such as this is paramount. Although the road is just down below you, a rescue here would be very difficult. We ask that first-time climbers go with a more experienced climber with a first-aid background. Youth and strength are no substitutes for the wisdom and knowledge that is acquired over years of climbing.

Split Rock

Located high above the Cannon Tram parking lot east of the parkway, this small crag is difficult to get to but features good climbing in a stunning alpine locale. The crag can be identified by the deep diagonal gash running through the cliff. Approach via the start of the Greenleaf Trail and after 100', bear left across a stream and follow ribbons up the left side of the drainage. When the ridge is reached and the angle decreases, head south for 300' until the bottom of the cliff is reached.

★ First Blood I 5.10a

1. Make difficult moves up a shallow groove on good rock (crux, 2 bolts), move left around a corner, then up a crack and reach a large white flake. Mantle over the flake and climb easier rock to a small pine tree. Surmount an awkward bulge, then climb corners to the top. Belay at small fir trees. 90'

Descent: A faint trail leads left (north) along the ridge-top and back down to the general area of the top of the drainage.

FA: Chuck Woodman and Dave Maheu August, 1996

Climbing routes on Hound's Hump Ridge

1. Alpine Breeze I 5.10
2. Too Old To Change I 5.10 R
3. Route 66 (with original start) II 5.8
4. New Variation start to Route 66 II 5.8
5. Revenge Is A Dish Best Served Cold II 5.8 R A2
6. Puckered Pork I 5.9+
7. Salted Packed Pig Sack I 5.8
8. Little Porky I 5.9
9. The West Chimney (Gully Variation start) I 5.6
10. The West Face I 5.8 R
11. Predator II 5.10d

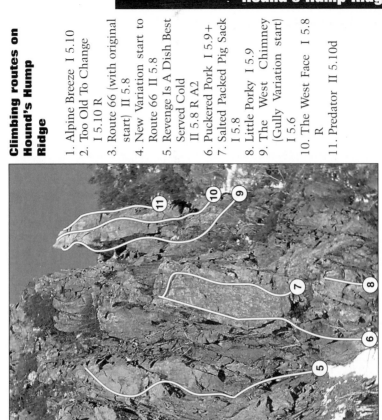

First Blood, Part Two I 5.10a A1

A more direct and harder finish to First Blood.

1a. Climb the first part of First Blood to a pine tree, then step right and move up to a large roof. Move left (A1) to a crack, and free-climb to the top. 90'

FA: Jon Sykes and Chuck Woodman June 12, 1997

The Dike I 5.4

The deep diagonal gash through the middle of the cliff is surprisingly easy yet very loose. Beware of the massive chalkstone at the top. 80'

FA: Unknown

Desperate Shortcoming I 5.10d (5.8 R)

On the far right side of Split Rock is an overhang six feet off the ground and a small horizontal crack just over the roof.

1. Pull the overhang (crux), protecting in the horizontal crack, then face climb (5.8 R) to a steep headwall with easy climbing leading to the top. 70'

FA: Jon Sykes and Chuck Woodman June 12, 1997

Hound's Hump Ridge: Eagle Crag Left

The Wing is a very large plate of rock standing some 100 feet tall, leaning against the main wall. Its distinguishing features are a finger crack up the middle of the face and a wider crack on its right side.

The approach has the same start as Split Rock. Park at the Cannon Tramway parking lot, Exit 2, I-93. Walk back and under the overpass to the start of the Greenleaf Trail. Follow trail for 300' until you see slabs leading to the ridge above. Bushwhack to the base of the slabs and either climb the slabs for two full pitches of 5.5 R to 5.6 R friction, or third class up a tree-filled ramp to the right of the slabs. Look for the Wing on your left, leaning against the main wall.

★ Broken Wing I 5.10c

The best finger crack on the ridge. Look in the center of The Wing for a striking vertical finger crack.

1. Climb crumbly rock a few feet until into the crack. Jam and layback up the crack to its end, then move diagonally right up to an arete and the top, or, alternately, climb directly above the crack past loose flakes at 5.11. 90', 5.10c

History: Chris Marks climbed the first ascent of the crack then moved right at the end, avoiding loose rock. Jon Sykes followed the route climbing directly above the crack at 5.11.
FA: Chris Marks and Jon Sykes August 15, 1996

★ Wing Ding   I 5.8

On the right side of The Wing is a hand crack that widens to body width near the top.
1. Climb the crack past a few small trees where the crack starts to widen, then climb the crack and arete to the top. 100'
FA: Jon Sykes and Chris Marks August 15, 1996

Several hundred feet right of The Wing is a distinct buttress with two 5.10 crack climbs on the front, and a two-pitch 5.8 on the right side. Access to these climbs is via the Eaglet Trail. When the trail meets the talus slope below the Eaglet, turn left and hike over to and around a low-angled buttress. Fourth class up the low-angled buttress 80' then traverse left to the base of the wall below the obvious cracks. (See Eaglet directions page 167.)

★ Alpine Breeze   I 5.10

This is the left crack. Alpine Breeze moves through a distinct overlap higher up the wall.
1. Climb up to the overlap, pull through it on its left and climb the crack system to the top. 140', 5.10
FRA: Paul Cormier and Jon Filmore-Patrick   September 1993 (Andy Tuthill recalls climbing this route with Chris Ellms many years before.)

★ Too Old To Change   I 5.10 R

Look for a small arete to the right-hand side of the overlap.
1. Climb the arete protecting high (5.10 R), step left and climb a faint crack system to the top. 140', 5.10 R   Rappel from bushes at the top; old slings were left in place.
FA: Paul Cormier and John Filmore-Patrick September 1993

★ Route 66   II 5.8

A two-pitch 5.8, called Route 66, starts on the south face of the buttress. Access is from the talus slope below Eaglet. Turn left and follow loose talus up into the gully between the buttress and the Flatiron. Look north at the south face of the buttress and you will see a distinct fractured crack system wandering up the wall. The old start is unprotected and loose, but Chuck Woodman cleaned and bolted (on the lead in August of 1999) a different start up a face left of the original first pitch. Rumor has it that the late John Waterman and/or Tom Lyman completed the first ascent in the 1970s. I found two rusted pins on the second pitch in 1995 while climbing with the late Bill Lowther. Both pins were removed easily with my fingers. Route description is to follow your nose for two pitches up a wonderful alpine crack system to the top. Rappelling is the only sane option down. Look for a fixed-pin belay on the top. There is a two-bolt belay on the top of the first pitch as well. Pitch one, 80'; pitch two, 140'

The next climb can be found up the gully, 100 feet right of Route 66. Just left of the Flatiron is a distinct gully that you third class up to a broken birch tree. Belay here. Facing north, you are now looking at an overhanging crack system in a left-facing corner. Revenge is a Dish Best Served Cold starts here, and the first two pitches are the best climbing. The third pitch is not recommended.

The author on the first pitch variation of Route 66   Jamie Cunningham

Revenge Is A Dish Best Served Cold II 5.8 R A2

1. Aid up past loose flakes (pin) to the crack, then follow the crack up to a small stance and belay off of one bolt stud and gear. 80', A2

2. Continue up the crack to its end and make a hard move onto a slab above. Now move up and left to a two-bolt belay on a pedestal of rock. (Beware of loose rock while moving across this slab.) 80', 5.8 A2

3. (Not Recommended) From the belay, climb up the extremely loose, run-out face above until you reach the bushes at the top. 60', 5.8 R

History: Jon Sykes and Gareth Slattery completed the first ascent of the first two pitches on a snow-covered 5th of April, 1996. Ice had to be removed from the crack for gear placements. This took a lot of time, and a subsequent rappel in the dark added to the experience. Jon Sykes and Jamie Cunningham added the third pitch on August 18th, 1996, in perfect weather.

Jamie Cunningham cleans the first pitch of Revenge Is A Dish Best Served Cold
Jon Sykes

The Flatiron

Surprisingly, this dramatic feature stood unclimbed until 1995, when I accepted the calling and completed the first ascent with the help of Chris Marks. Two wonderful routes now exist on the Flatiron that add greatly to the number of quality alpine routes in this remote setting.

The approach is via the Eaglet Trail. When you finally meet the talus slope below the Eaglet, turn left after fifty feet, and follow looser talus up and left to the base of the Flatiron. Puckered Pork starts here and weaves its way up the left side of the main face.

★ Puckered Pork I 5.9+

This route is not for the timid. Although it is mostly bolt-protected, there are healthy run-outs between the bolts. The climb requires smaller natural gear and starts at a lone bolt fifteen feet up on a small overlap.

1. Climb face and cracks to an overlap, then pull the overlap (bolt) and climb steep face past a hidden pin and up to a ledge. Step right onto the main face and ascend the wall past four bolts to the top. Belay at a two-bolt anchor. 160', 5.9+

History: After a prior attempt with help from Chris Marks (when Jon Sykes led a variation finish at 5.9 X), Sykes later rope-soloed and bolted two thirds of the climb. Jon Sykes and Chris Marks made the first complete ascent of the route on July 5, 1995.

★ Salt Packed Pig Sack I 5.8

This is one of the finest 5.8 face climbs in the Notch. The protection is good and the vantage point is incredible. From the start of Puckered Pork, third class up the corner to the top of a broken buttress, and belay here at a bolt and fixed hex. The climb follows the right side of the main face. The start is protected by two bolts, and small natural gear is needed throughout the climb.

1. Face-climb past two bolts and one pin up horizontal edges to a hollow flake on your right. Then continue above past two more bolts and the top. 120', 5.8

FA: Jon Sykes and Chris Marks Spring 1995

History: Jon Sykes rope-soloed up to the third bolt before running out of daylight. He then returned the next day and, with the help of Chris Marks, completed the first ascent. The name refers to a story Jon told Chris about neutering piglets as a youngster.

Little Porky I 5.9

At the front bottom of the Salt Packed Pig Sack buttress is a broken crack system. Approach via the Eaglet talus slope.

1. Start at the bottom right side of the buttress and follow the broken crack system up onto the front face and the top of the buttress. 60', 5.9

History: Jon Sykes and Bill Keiler top-roped the route in the spring of 1996. Jon returned a week later and rope-soloed the first ascent.

The author seconds one of his favorite routes—Salt Packed Pig Sack—on the Flatiron
Mike Lee

Hound's Hump Ridge: Eagle Crag Center

The next climb mentioned in this section is on the wall left of Eaglet Spire.

Approaching the Eaglet is now much easier. While driving through the Notch, get off Exit 2 (Cannon Tram Exit) and park at the Old Man viewing lot. (There is a gift shop and ice cream parlor to cool you down after a long day of cragging.) Walk down the bike path (south) a few hundred feet and turn left at the tiny log cabin and walk under the overpass to the north-bound side of the highway. Walk down the bike path 50' and you will come to a curve in the path. The Eaglet Trail starts here on your left and passes several large boulders at the beginning of the trail. Several hundred feet in, you will come to a boulder and a decomposed bench, right beside the trail. Behind the bench, the trail continues up and meets the Greenleaf Trail. It crosses the Greenleaf Trail at a cairn and continues up fairly directly until you meet the talus slope below the Eaglet. Follow the talus up, staying right of the Eaglet until below the spire's south wall. It takes about half an hour to reach the Eaglet. The first climb described is located on the wall behind and left of the spire.

Unnamed I 5.9

Looking at the Eaglet's south wall from the talus-sloped trail, you'll see a short steep trail just to the left of the spire. This trail accesses both the west chimney's second pitch on the right, and an unnamed route on the left (about 80'). Look for a broken, right-facing corner.

1. Climb the corner past blocks until you reach a final headwall. The route follows a pin on the right to the top and was most likely aided originally. Gareth Slattery led the corner to the top at 5.9, climbing past loose rock and sketchy protection (1998).

FA: Unknown

The Eaglet

The most prominent free-standing spire on the east coast, the Eaglet has a long history dating back to 1929. The first ascentist down-climbed from the adjacent cliff into the notch and gained the summit. Lincoln O' Brien and Robert Underhill achieved the summit in May, 1929. The Eaglet and the surrounding crags makes this area a destination unto itself. Aid climbs and free climbs of all difficulties can be found here. Please be mindful of where you are when climbing in this remote alpine arena. Loose rock and a hard approach imply commitment and self-reliance. Make sure others know where you are and when you're expected back. Also, carry rain gear, a first aid kit, and extra clothing in case of an unexpected weather change.

Peregrine Falcon Alert!

Though no longer listed as an endangered species, the Peregrine Falcon is still protected to ensure full recovery of this magnificent bird of prey. The Peregrine's nesting sites change from year to year between the Eaglet and Eagle Cliff (and sometimes Cannon). Signs will be posted on the trail if the birds are nesting on either cliff. We ask that you do not climb anywhere that is posted from April 1st to August 1st.

The Eaglet routes will be described from left to right, starting with the West Chimney and ending with The Old Route.

★ The West Chimney I 5.6 [Original Start 5.7]

This is the best intermediate climb on the Eaglet. The original route starts on the southwest corner of the spire. When approaching the spire from the trail, you will come to the base of the south wall. Walk left twenty feet to the southwest corner. Two climbs start here with the corner to your right being Peregrine Arete (5.9+) and the West Chimney on your left. The original start can be avoided on the left by scrambling up a short trail/gully to the start of the second pitch chimney.

1. Climb a fractured bulge past a pin and move left across a smooth slab, then up a small inside corner and the trees. (Beware of loose rock.) 80', 5.7
2. Wedge your way up the right-hand of two parallel chimneys past a large chalkstone to a comfortable ledge. Belay here, or keep climbing to the summit past an old bolt and the top. 120', 5.6

History: A Swiss ski instructor, Peter Gabriel, who was employed by Cannon Mountain Ski Area, completed the first ascent in 1930 with M. Leiper and D. Miller, Jr.

The West Face I 5.8 R

This is the face just right of the West Chimney. I climbed this route in the early 1990s and found a pin near the top. Protection can be found in horizontal and vertical cracks scattered along the climb. Start at West Chimney's first pitch, then take the line of least resistance up the face to the top.

FA: Unknown

★ Peregrine Arete II 5.9+

This is a burly route best climbed with double ropes and a steady mind. Ironically, there is very little arete climbing involved, mostly crack and face climbing. The crux for me requires a head smear into the corner crack—classic alpine fun!

Start just right of the first pitch of the West Chimney. Double ropes are mandatory for maximum enjoyment.

1. Climb thin cracks and flakes straight up past pins to a slab below an overhang. Face climb up and right (bolt) of the overhang and undercling right on a hanging flake to an overhanging right-facing corner/crack.

Climb the crack (crux) past a pin to a small stance and belay. 90', 5.9+

2. Climb up a few feet and diagonally right past two narrow ledges and climb a short headwall (pin) to a ledge and a belay. Or keep climbing to the top and belay. 120'

FA: Ed Webster, Rope-solo October, 1986

★ Predator II 5.10d

This recent addition to the Eaglet is the hardest free climb on the spire. Primarily bolt-protected, it does require some natural protection. Start ten feet right of Peregrine Arete on the overhanging south wall.

1. Climb suspect flakes to a pin, then step left and ascend thin cracks up to and past a bolt on its left. Steep, thin face-climbing takes you to the next bolt and the crux of the climb. Pull a small overlap (5.10d), or traverse left from the bolt to a large flake and pull up onto a ledge (5.10c), with big fall potential. Above is the overhanging corner/crack of Peregrine Arete. Climb the corner and belay on a small stance. 80', 5.10d (or 5.10c)

2. Traverse left a few feet to the first bolt on pitch two. Now climb as directly as possible up the arete, following a line of bolts to the top. Some natural gear is needed and one more bolt will be placed on the arete to keep the line from wandering. 80', 5.10b

FA: Brad White, Dick Peterson, and Ian Cruickshank Late 1980s

★ August Child II 5.8 A4

This is the hardest aid climb on the eastern side of the Notch. Micro nailing on this overhung bad-dog is nothing short of religious. Start eight feet right of Predator at a discontinuous seam, and weave through the overhanging south wall. Peckers, RURPS, hooks, and bashies are needed.

1. The start is climbed free with little protection until you reach the seam 15 feet up. Now start nailing and hooking up the seam until it ends at a fractured bulge. Free-climb (5.8) over the bulge diagonally right (loose rock) to a short right-facing corner. Ascend the corner to a large belay ledge just below the top. 120', 5.8 A4

History: Jon Sykes completed the first ascent rope-solo on August 9, 1997, naming the route after friends Gareth and Nicole Slattery's first child, Logan, who was born the day before.

The East Chimney II 5.7

The least-climbed of the routes on the Eaglet, this route needs cleaning and some tender, loving care.

1. Forty feet left of Old Route is a chimney a little wider than a body with a couple of chalk stones wedged in it. The East Chimney climbs this up to the Notch and connects with the Old Route.

FA: Earle Whipple and Jim Hebert June 14, 1964

The Old Route I 5.6

This was the first climb on the Eaglet to start from the bottom. It used to be called the Standard Route, but it has been renamed because the first pitch gully is very loose and unappealing and thus is no longer the standard route. The West Chimney is the best moderate route and gets my recommendation.

1. Climb the gully up past pins (loose rock) trending left up the notch and a fixed belay. 110', 5.5

2. There are two ways to the summit from here; the first is via the left side of the face. Climb the steep face past a hidden piton, then up to a ledge and a couple moves to the spire's top. Or climb the top of the West Chimney. 40', 5.6 Rappel off the summit bolts with 60-meter doubles down the overhung south face or down to the notch and to the ground via two rappels down the east side.

History: On May 24, 1930, Kenneth Henderson, Ledyard Stebbins, Dana Durand, and friends completed the first ascent from the bottom.

The Long Wall

Located just up the hill behind the Eaglet is an attractive 250-foot wall that has long captured the eyes of climbers perched atop the popular Eaglet Spire. Three routes are found on this face. The first route, which starts in the gully (same start as Old Route), is undocumented and was probably climbed in the 1970s. A large stopper with 8mm perlon was found on the 5.9 crux, and a rusted pin was found on the upper pitch. There is now a direct start at A3 just right of the gully.

Land of the Pebble People II 5.9 A3

This is the direct start to an old route. The old start up the gully to the right is 5.5 and loose.

1. Five feet right of Old Route gully are stacked blocks leading to a short

Long Wall and Gully Wall climbing routes

1. The West Face I 5.8 R (Eaglet)
2. Predator II 5.10d (Eaglet)

Long Wall

3. The Old Route start of the Eaglet, and an unnamed route heading up the left side of the Long Wall 5.7
4. Land of the Pebble People II 5.9 A3
5. Birdland II 5.11b
6. Shortcut to a Religious Experience I 5.7 R

Gully Wall

7. Project
8. Dodo Man I 5.8 A3
9. Ugly Clean Through I 5.8 A3 (not seen in photo)

left-facing corner. Climb the corner (pin) to its top, then aid a seam on your left up to a ledge. The original route connects here from the gully. Now climb up through a slightly overhung crack system (loose rock) to a small belay ledge. 120', 5.9 A3 (or 5.9)

2. Follow cracks and face up line of least resistance to the top. 100', 5.6

History: Jon Sykes and Chris Marks made the first ascent of the direct start on September 13, 1997. No information is known of the original route.

The following climb weaves a fairly direct line up the full length of the wall's right side. Approach by continuing up past the Eaglet until a very loose scree slope leading up to the ridge is reached. The route can be viewed from the open slope. Locate the bolt anchor at the top of the first pitch and head to the bottom of the wall directly below the anchor.

★ Birdland   II 5.11b

1. Climb a thin crack in an overhanging wall (crux, pins) to a stance below a right-leaning crack in a corner. Follow the crack, then pull over a bulge (large cam) and climb a sparsely protected groove over moderate rock to a two-bolt anchor and comfortable stance. 90'

2. Beautiful face climbing (5.9) leads up and left across an arete to a hidden ledge. Climb straight up over moderate rock past a bolt and pins and the occasional loose block to a two-bolt anchor on the right. This is a spectacular pitch. 110'

3. Climb easily up and right over a sharp, low-angle arete to blueberry bushes and the trail. 60'

Descend via either a spectacular 120' rappel from fixed anchors down the very steep gully wall to the east, or continue past the rappel anchors on a good trail to the col and top of the aforementioned scree slope. Descend loose scree to the vicinity of the Eaglet.

History: Chuck Woodman and Dave Maheu completed pitch one in August of 1997, just before Maheu moved to Colorado. Woodman returned in September to complete pitch two with Steve Dupuis, then returned in October with Mark Hall to finish the route.

Shortcut to a Religious Experience   I 5.7 R

The third route on the Long Wall is on the very right edge of the Wall. Shortcut to A Religious Experience weaves its way up a fishhook ridge in one long 60-meter pitch. Hike up past Birdland twenty-five feet to the start of the ridge.

FA: Gareth Slattery and Jon Sykes Summer, 1998

Gully Wall

The steepest face on the eastern side of the notch only has two routes and both are A3. There is also a free-climbing project in progress in the center of the face. Keep following the very loose talus slope up past Long Wall to just below the gully leading to the col.

★ Dodo Man I 5.8 A3

Just right of center is a broken mini-buttress leading to a faint seam. Start by climbing the buttress.

1. Climb the broken buttress up to a left diagonal ramp. The ramp moves left and you climb straight up past a hidden pin in a pocket. Then follow faint seam (rivet) up to a small stance and a bolt. Traverse right, then up to a undercling crack which you climb back left then straight up to the top. 120', 5.8 A3

History: Jon Sykes made the first ascent rope-solo in two pushes without fixed ropes. On the first attempt he ran out of daylight. He then returned on May 14, 1997, and completed the route. Two falls were taken on the second attempt before reaching the high point of the first attempt.

Ugly Clean Through I 5.8 A3

On the very right side of the Gully Wall is a fractured overhang system. This is an extremely loose climb that I do not recommend unless you have a deathwish, in which case, have at it.

1. Climb a loose flake system up to a point below the first roof. Nail out left under first roof (pin) until you can pull the roof. Now climb up to a second roof, pulling it, and free climb to the top.

FA: Jon Sykes and Steve Dupuis May 25, 1997

Climbers have been seen on the green wall to the right of Garcia Vega, a winter ice climb two hundred feet right (south) of the col. No information is known about routes in this area.

Jamie Cunningham

Hound's Hump Ridge in winter from Cannon Mountain Ski Area

Eagle Cliff

Located high on the western flanks of Mt. Lafayette, Eagle Cliff commands a view of Franconia Notch State Park's impressive glacial passage. From this vantage point the sight of Cannon Cliff across the Notch is magnificent. Because of Cannon's dominance as the climbing destination in the Notch, crags like Eagle Cliff have been ignored almost completely. The first known ascent of the cliff was not until the 1970s when a young Johnny Waterman stepped up to the task. Following the obvious dike system up and through the immense diagonal overhang for three pitches, Waterman established the very first route, rated then at 5.7 (old school). Ken Query and Guy Waterman climbed the route in the eighties and commented on its difficulty and how much loose rock there was to contend with. This is typical of that section of the cliff.

There are fifteen known routes on Eagle Cliff, including one mixed rock and ice climb. Routes will be described from right to left (south to north) as you approach the cliff from the Greenleaf Trail.

Directions: Leave your car at the Cannon Tram parking lot and walk back and under the Interstate 93 overpass to the start of the Greenleaf Trail. Follow the Greenleaf Trail for approximately one and a half miles until just before a distinct pass, known to locals as Eagle Pass. Look for an overgrown trail on your left and follow this to the base of the cliff's south side. Luck of the Green is the first climb you see.

★ Luck of the Green I 5.12a/b

As the trail meets the cliff, look for a roof twenty feet off the ground and a crack above it leading to face climbing. This is the hardest free climb on Eagle Cliff.

1. Climb past three bolts and hollow flakes through the roof. Then follow a crack (pin) above to face climbing and one final death flake that can be avoided on the right. Bolt and pin belay. 100'

FA: Jon Sykes, Bill Kieler, and Bill Rzepa March 17, 1996
FFA: Jon Sykes and Randy Garcia August 5, 2000

★ Wet Shoes, Sound Mind I 5.9

Start twenty feet left (north) of Luck of the Green, at a bolt ten feet off the ground leading to a vertical crack.

1. Climb up and left of bolt to the crack, then follow the crack to a ledge and step right and ascend an arete to a bolt and sling belay. 100'

FA: Jon Sykes, rope-solo August 27, 1998

★ I'll Lead That II 5.10c (5.9 R)

This is a hidden gem worth seeking out.

Follow ramp left forty-feet past Wet Shoes, Sound Mind, and belay below and right of a lone bolt protecting the first moves of the climb.

1. Climb up and left of the bolt to a V-notch (pin). Jam the crack in the corner up to a small stance and belay here. 60', 5.8

2. Move up flakes to a gently overhung wall with a finger crack. Climb the crack and face and trend left near the top to a fixed belay. 60', 5.10c (5.9 R)

FA: Jon Sykes and Gareth Slattery August, 1995
FFA: Jon Sykes and Bill Keiler March 19, 1996

★ Zion Dreaming I 5.8 A3

Although the first part is hard to discern, the crack above is not. Walking north from the previous route, you will come to a small clearing with stacked stones. Zion Dreaming and Meister Shooter start here.

1. Climb the crack and flake until on top of the flake (loose rock). From here aid diagonally left (A3) to a right-facing corner. Move up the corner, then step left and into a diagonal crack, and climb it to a two-bolt belay. 140'

FA: Jon Sykes and Steve Dupuis March 30, 1997

Eagle Cliff climbing routes

1. Shape Shifters III 5.8 A4 (unfinished)
2. The Waterman Dike II 5.8
3. New Kids on the Rock I 5.9
4 Stoned Fingers with Hidden Treasure start II 5.11
5. Land of the Unknown I 5.10b (5.9 R)
6. The Late Show I 5.11d
7. Farewell Chris I 5.11d (5.9 R)
8. Farewell Angelina I 5.11d
9. Meister Shooter I 5.8 A2
10. Zion Dreaming I 5.8 A3
11. I'll Lead That II 5.10c (5.9 R)
12 Wet Shoes, Sound Mind I 5.9
13. Luck of the Green I 5.12a/b

★ Meister Shooter I 5.8 A2

On the upper wall is a striking seam/crack that weaves its way up through an overhanging scoop to produce Meister Shooter. Start ten feet left of Zion in a broken right-facing corner.

1. Climb the corner past a pin and up to a bolt beside a loose block and pull onto the main face. Move up the face and cracks to the start of the main crack. Move your way up the incredible crack to its end and make some tricky free moves around the bulge to a two-bolt belay. Rappel with two ropes. 130′

FA: Jon Sykes and Steve Dupuis July 22, 1996

★ Farewell Angelina I 5.11d

This is the first modern sport/traditional hard-man route on Eagle Cliff, put up by Joe TerraVecchia and Karin Bates in 1992. 5.11d sport and 5.11 crack climbing make this the most sustained route on the cliff. Forty feet left (north) of Meister is a line of four bolts leading to a crack. Step up and fire away. There is an easier start at the Late Show that diagonals from left to right into the crack at 5.9.

1. Climb a steep face past four bolts to a crack with a wide start. Ascend the crack and face to a two-bolt belay. 130′

FA: Joe TerraVecchia and Karin Bates 1992

Farewell Chris I 5.11d (5.9 R)

1. Start at Farewell Angelina and step right at the crack and climb the thin seam past loose flakes with micro wires and cams.

History: Chris Marks and Jon Sykes climbed this variation avoiding Farewell Angelina's upper crack. Chris' lead was one of the best on-sight trad leads I've ever seen.

FA: Chris Marks and Jon Sykes Summer, 1998

★ The Late Show I 5.11d or 5.10d

Twenty feet left (north) of previous route is a line of bolts weaving up a golden wall. Another classic climb by TerraVecchia and Bates.

1. Climb thin, bolted face up to overhang, then pull overhang directly at 5.11d, or just left at 5.10d, past more bolts and then ascend discontinuous cracks to a two-bolt belay. Bring small to medium gear. 130′

History: TerraVecchia led the route just as the sun was setting, and as a result, Joe and his partner spent the next two hours groveling down the trail without headlamps. The sky was ink black so they used the flash on

Chris Marks
leads
the incredibly
sustained
Late Show

Jamie Cunningham

the camera to illuminate the trail. They got back twenty or so tree shots to remember the day by and made it to the bar in Franconia at 10 p.m. to meet some friends.

FA: Joe TerraVecchia and Karin Bates 1997

Land of the Unknown I 5.10b [5.9 R]

Between The Late Show and Hidden Treasure is a steep face marked with a lone bolt sixty feet up, and a pin above leading past an old fixed RP wire nut. Climb to a two-bolt belay on Hidden Treasure.

FA: Unknown
FFA: Chris Marks and Jon Sykes August 26, 2000

★ Hidden Treasure I 5.9

Peek around the corner and you will find Hidden Treasure. Just left of The Late Show is a hidden left-facing corner.

1. Climb the corner to its end (bolt) then diagonal up and right to another corner (bolt). Belay here. 5.9

2. Stem and jam up the next corner on very enjoyable climbing to a two-bolt belay. Can be led in one pitch. 5.9

FA: Joe TerraVecchia and David Denny 1985

Eric Pospesil leads the first pitch of Hidden Treasure/Stone Fingers
Jamie Cunningham

Jamie Cunningham follows
the first pitch of
Stoned Fingers

Lois LaRock

★ Stoned Fingers II 5.11b (5.8 R)

This is the directissima of Eagle Cliff with a colorful history and virtuoso climbing on the first two pitches. Start on Hidden Treasure and follow bolts straight up a steep face.

1. Climb Hidden Treasure corner to its top (bolt), then face climb up a steep wall past widely spaced bolts and occasional cracks to an alcove and a two-bolt belay. 5.9
2. Step left from alcove and climb a steep face past a bolt to a crack. Ascend the crack past two fixed pins (crux), and make a hard exit from the crack to small corners (loose) and the belay. 5.11b
3. Climb directly above belay to a steep short wall. Step right and climb dark corner up and left to an obvious cleft, then follow ramp (5.8 R) up left to its end and a bolt and pin belay.

History: In the summer of 1995, Jon Sykes and Jamie Cunningham camped at the base of Eagle Cliff with the intention of completing a new route. Late on the second day Jamie was on the lead working out the last pitch when he dislodged a 200-pound boulder onto his chest crushing two of his fingers on his left hand. The boulder then proceeded on a direct path toward the belay, narrowly missing the rope and cutting my leg with shrapnel from the impact of the boulder eight inches away. First aid was administered and a self-rescue took two hours to get Jamie down and to the hospital. The route was finished the very next day with Chris Marks finishing the last pitch.

FA: Jon Sykes, Jamie Cunningham, and Chris Marks Summer, 1995
FA: Direct Second Pitch: Jon Sykes and Chris Marks August 1, 1997

New Kids on the Rock I 5.9

This is the most recent addition to Eagle Cliff and very alpine. Start 25 feet left (north) of Stoned Fingers at a blocky left-facing corner.

1. Climb corner system to top of buttress. Move left onto sloping ledge below dike. Climb up and left onto face. Continue to large belay ledge on left with two-bolt anchor.

2. Step right and climb face/arete to large block. Jamb fist/hand crack to top of block. Belay on edge below right facing open book.

3. To be continued

FRA: First pitch: Shad and Janel Lawton, Jamie Cunningham, and Jon Sykes June 24, 2000
FRA: Second pitch: Shad and Janel Lawton August 26, 2000
History: Andy Tuthill recalls climbing this line to about the same high point back in the 1980s.

The Waterman Dike II 5.8

What is the first thing a climber will see when gazing up at Eagle Cliff? A distinct dike system cutting through the immense diagonal overhang. John Waterman was so impressed with the line that he had to climb it. Sometime in the early 1970s, Waterman, with an unknown partner, completed the first ascent of the route. The start is a bit vague, but look for a gully with a broken buttress on its right about 100 feet left of New Kids on the Rock. Climb up and right into the dike proper, then ascend the dike for two more pitches and the top. Loose rock is everywhere on this section of the cliff, so care is needed if you want to survive.

FA: John Waterman and partner Early 1970s

Shad Lawton on New
Kids On The Rock

Mike Lee

Shape Shifters III 5.8 A4 (unfinished)

This route starts in the same gully as The Waterman Dike but follows the left side of the gully instead.

1. Climb into the gully and step to the left side (north) of the gully. Ascend a corner system up (loose rock) until you make awkward moves onto a pedestal and a two-bolt belay. 5.6

2. Step right from the belay and weave your way up under a huge roof on thin nailing and hooking, then climb out the left side of the roof and pull through a V-notch that leads to a ledge and a two-bolt belay. 5.8 A4

3. One more pitch leads to the top and is yet to be completed.

History: Jon Sykes and Steve Dupuis made the first ascent of the first two pitches on a cold, snow-covered 26th of April in 1998. They made it to the ledge on the second pitch in the dark and got back to the cars at 10 p.m. Of equal note, in a Herculean effort, Mike Lee hiked to the top of Eagle Cliff and rappeled down the face to take photographs of the first ascent. There is no way to describe how thick and impenetrable the bushes are at the top.

FA: First two pitches: Jon Sykes and Steve Dupuis April 26, 1998

Steve Dupuis tries to stay warm at the first pitch belay of Shape Shifters during the first ascent

Mike Lee

The author leads the A4 section under the roof of Shape Shifters
Mike Lee

Indian Head

Standing at the Indian Head Resort on Route 3, look west, and lo and behold you will find another incredible profile. Although very little has been climbed at Indian Head, there are infinite possibilities. The routes that do exist are hard to find, and very few people even bother. As you approach on Route 3, there is a small parking lot across the road and down from the Flume Visitor's Center south of Franconia Notch State Park. Park here and walk west on a marked trail that takes you directly to the top of Indian Head. Look for two forty-foot finger cracks with the same start. The left crack is 5.10, and the right side is 5.10+. Rappel or scramble down to the base and the start of these and other climbs.

Bitch 5.7+
1. Find the short, overhung off-width crack on the left side of the cliff.
FA: Jim Graham and Bill Coffey September 10, 1983

★ Skookum Roof 5.10+
This is the best route at Indian Head, if you can find it.
1. Ascend the overhanging chimney up to a fifteen-foot roof. Then out the roof via cracks on either side of the roof. 80′, 5.10+
FA: Steve Larson and Andy Tuthill September, 1982

Red Power 5.10+
Start twenty-five feet right of Skookum Roof and just left of a bottomless, left-facing corner twenty feet up.
1. Climb a steep face up to a corner, then up to a small belay ten feet above the corner. 5.10+
2. Keep following the corner until you can walk off left. Instead, step right and climb the steep crack to the top. 100′, 5.8
FA: Steve Larson and Andy Tuthill September, 1982

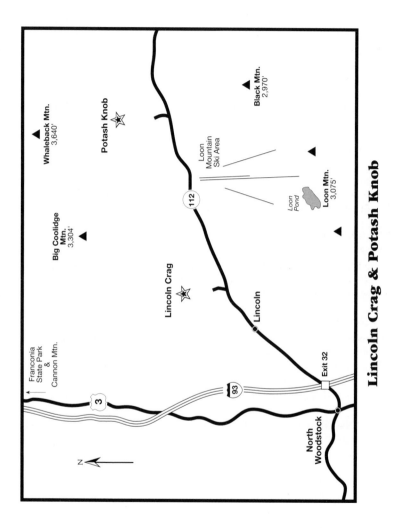

Lincoln Crag & Potash Knob

Lincoln Crag

Lincoln Crag (or First Ledge) has always been enjoyed by local residents. Starting with an easy hike, it offers rewarding views to the south and a very peaceful setting. In winter it is a popular place to snowshoe and cross country ski. Lincoln resident Dr. Dana Bartlett and his family spent quite a bit of time on the hill cleaning and top-roping some of the more obvious faces. In the past couple of years, the area has seen more development. Climbs have been established on lead and given ratings based on local consensus.

How to get there: From exit 32 off Interstate 93, drive east towards Loon Mountain for 1.6 miles. Take a left turn at the sign for Forest Ridge Development (Kancamagus Rec. Road). Drive past the Lin-Wood Town Park and continue up the hill into Forest Ridge. At the top of the hill the road will bend to the left and there will be a large stone wall directly in front of you. Park at the end in the Sports Club parking lot and walk back to the stone wall you just passed. The trail begins at the end of the wall and heads up behind it. Stay on the trail for a couple of minutes and you will come to a fork. Here you want to stay to the right and start heading up the hill through some talus. When you come to another small landing the trail will split again. Heading left and over the footbridge will take you through all the cliffs, while going straight up the hill will lead you past Middle Ledge and to the top of First Ledge.

Please note: All access to this area is through private property. Please be respectful of the homeowners by not parking in the condo parking spaces. Park in the Sports Club parking lot or at the Town Park at the bottom of the hill. Please pick up any trash you may see along the trail and keep your dogs on a leash until you get some distance up the trail.

WARNING: We are not the only people who use this area. Unfortunately several rappel anchors have been vandalized. All fixed anchors should be inspected!

Lincoln Crag offers mostly traditional and mixed climbing and a few sport routes, although a basic leader's rack should be carried on all routes. The route descriptions start from the footbridge at the Lower Slab and continue up the trail.

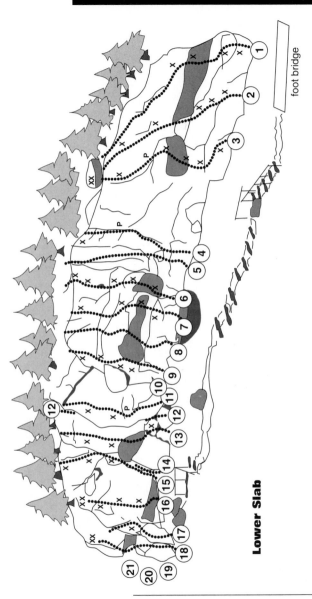

Lower Slab

foot bridge

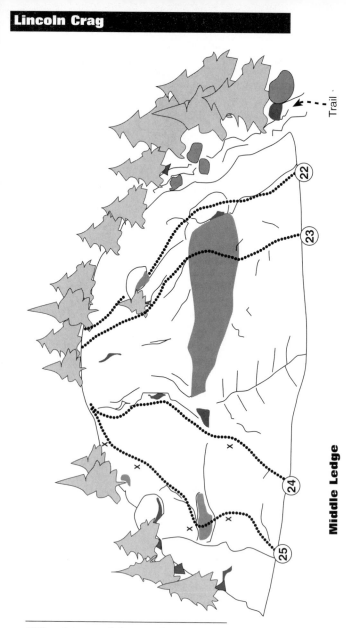

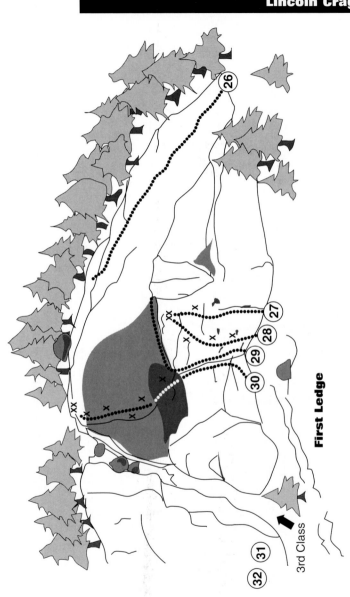

First Ledge

3rd Class

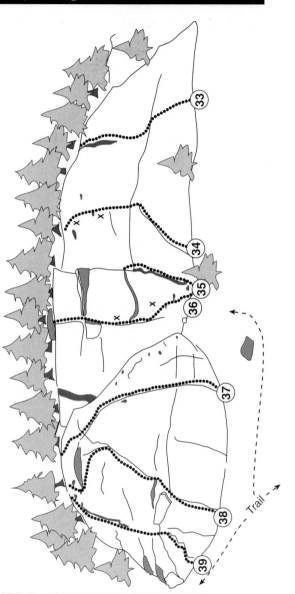

Upper Cliff

Route listings for Lincoln Crag

Lower Slab

1. Rain Delay 5.7+
2. Ninety Degrees in
   the Shade 5.7
3. Trick or Treat 5.8+ (5.5 R)
4. Lucky Pierre 5.10b
5. Scorpion 5.9
6. Kai's Arete (a.k.a. Shovelhead)
   5.10c
7. Good To Go 5.8+
8. Psycho Babble 5.10b
9. Octoberfest 5.9
10. Hand Jive 5.9
11. Twisted Schister 5.10a
12. Crooked Corner 5.7
13. Face Off 5.10a
14. Schoolhouse Rock 5.6
15. Black Fly Festival 5.11d/5.12a
16. Start Me Up 5.8+
17. Race Day 5.7
18. The Wicked Roof (Project)
19. Squirrel Meat
    (a.k.a. Omnivore) 5.10b
20. Bombs Away 5.10a
21. Rocket 5.10d

Middle Ledge

22. 5.9 Project
23. 5.10/5.11 Project
24. Shoot Up or Shut Up 5.10b
25. Free For All 5.10c

First Ledge

26. Little Feat 5.9+
27. Hunchback Crack 5.10a
28. Thin Lizzy 5.9+
29. Frosted Flake 5.7
30. Stiff Little Fingers 5.10d/5.11a
31. Crescent Moon 5.5
32. Green Line 5.6

Upper Cliff

33. Mossy Madness 5.7
34. Fatty Acid (a.k.a. Second
    Time's a Winner) 5.9+
35. Strange Days 5.6
36. Amino Maker 5.9+
37. Mexican Radio 5.7
38. Free Clinic 5.7

Lower Slab

Rain Delay 5.7+

At the footbridge, the first climb you come to is an obvious bulge with two bolts. Climb past the bolts and into an easy crack system, heading towards the far right corner. Pull over the tricky overhang past two more bolts, and follow the slab and horizontal cracks to the top. Belay at the fixed anchor. (150') Exit left and rappel Good to Go; one rope. 4 bolts/nuts, cams to #3
FA: Brian Whitfield and Kai Poesse June, 1999

★ Ninety Degrees in the Shade 5.7

Starting just to the left of Rain Delay, climb the moderate slab past three bolts and head straight to the crack system in the corner above you. Follow the crack system up and over (crux) on good pro, and move towards the bolt above. Easier moves with adequate pro lead to the fixed anchor above. (150') Exit left off Good to Go. 4 bolts/nuts, cams to #3
FA: Brian Whitfield and Kai Poesse June, 1999

★ Trick or Treat 5.8+ (5.5 R)

Fifteen feet beyond the footbridge, look for the obvious strip of cleaned rock and a finger crack. Move up through shelfy slabs (5.5 R) to a large ledge. Small friction holds lead to bomber holds over the large bulge (crux) and a ledge above. Head up the open book past a bolt, then move right towards the boulder and the fixed anchor. (140') Rappel off of Good to Go.
5 bolts, piton, nuts/cams to #2.5
FA: Brian Whitfield and Kai Poesse October, 1998

Lucky Pierre 5.10b

Climb past an overgrown ledge and slightly right past a couple of fixed pins. Continue up on nice rock into the right one of two corners. Mantle past a pin and move left to clip a bolt at the top. Belay at the tree.
1 bolt, pitons, nuts/cams to #2
FA: Chuck Woodman and Pierre Girouard October, 1998

Scorpion 5.9

Climb past the grassy ledge, then left, to the left corner of the two parallel corners. Stem up to clip a pin, then make thin moves up the clean corner past a small stump at the top. Belay at the fixed anchor. 65'
Piton, nuts/cams to #2
FA: Chuck Woodman and Pierre Girouard October, 1998

Mike "Bubba" Lee
leads Trick Or Treat
on the
Lower Slab

Jon Sykes

★ Kai's Arete (a.k.a. Shovelhead) 5.10c

At the top of the steps, move right onto the grassy ledge, and belay at the
tree. Step up to clip the first bolt, then make a powerful reach up into the
flake and follow good holds past two more bolts to a mantle move onto a
ledge. At the ledge, protect with a nut or small cam. Thin face moves lead
past two more bolts to the top. Belay at the tree. 60′
5 bolts, nuts/small TCUs
FA: Kai Poesse and Brian Whitfield September, 1999

Jamie Cunningham follows Kai's Arete a.k.a. Shovelhead   Jon Sykes

★ Good to Go 5.8+

From the grassy ledge, climb up past a large stump in a wide crack to a
steep shallow corner with two bolts. Climb past the bolts and mantle onto
the ledge. A crack system continues up to a final bolt and the tricky mantle over the top. Belay at the tree. 60′
3 bolts, nuts/cams to #2
FA: Chuck Woodman and Pierre Girouard September, 1998

★ Psycho Babble 5.10b

Just to the left of Good to Go, climb up a flake to the horizontal crack.
Power over the roof on thin pro, then move towards the headwall and
climb the broken crack system on good holds over the top. 60′
Nuts/cams to #2.5
FA: Jon Sykes and Chris Marks May, 1999

★ Octoberfest 5.9

Step off a stone and on to a large flake. Move up on tricky holds past two
bolts and onto a sloping ledge. Move slightly left and up on sloping holds
to the top. 45′, 5 bolts
FA: Brian Whitfield and Kai Poesse October, 1998

Randy Garcia
pulling the second
ascent of Psycho
Babble

Jon Sykes

Hand Jive 5.9+
Start at the upper right corner of a nice clean face, near some wedged blocks. Follow the obvious, left-leaning hand/finger crack to the top. 45′
FA: Brian Whitfield and Kai Poesse July, 1998

★ Twisted Schister 5.10a
At the lower left-hand corner of the clean face, start near the base of a huge pine tree. Move up on nice features with some natural pro to a fixed pin. Go straight up the face past two bolts to the top. For an easier finish (5.8), from the pin, move left up the arete (clipping the bolts) to the belay ledge. 50′ 2 bolts, piton, nuts/cams to #2
FA: Chuck Woodman and Dana Bartlett August, 1995

★ Crooked Corner 5.7

Around the corner to the left of Twisted Schister, start into a crack system in some large broken boulders and onto a sloping ledge. Stem up the corner and onto a belay ledge. 50′ Nuts/cams to #2

FA Brian Whitfield and Kai Poesse August, 1998

★ Face Off 5.10a

Start into the same crack system as Crooked Corner and move onto the sloping ledge. Move left towards the bolts on the upper face. Start up the face just to the left of the bolts, and reach for a good hold on the arete. Move back onto the face past the second bolt, and climb straight up to the ledge. 60′ Rap off the tree. 3 bolts, nuts/cams

FA: Brian Whitfield and Kai Poesse August, 1998

Schoolhouse Rock 5.6

Climb the obvious right slanting hand crack to the left of Face Off. Fun moves lead over a small ledge, then follow the crack to the top. Good pro! (45′) Nuts/cams to #3

FA: Kai Poesse and Brian Whitfield August, 1998

★ Black Fly Festival 5.11d/5.12a

Start just to the left of the chimney and move up under the overhang to a bolt. Mantle onto the ledge and climb into the corner above, then left and onto the steep headwall. Three bolts lead up the wall to a very cruxy finish. 50′ 4 bolts, nuts/cams to #2.5

FA: Jon Sykes and Brian Whitfield June, 1999

Start Me Up 5.8+

Start just to the right of a low, right-slanting roof. Move up and left on tricky holds past three bolts to the top.
Rap the route or walk off. 40′ 3 bolts

FA: Brian Whitfield and Kai Poesse July, 1998

Race Day 5.7

Climb a short face to an open book with a single bolt. Pull over the ledge to a small tree with an anchor. Rap off the route. 35′ 1 bolt, nuts/cams to #2

FA: Chuck Woodman May, 1999

The author on the
first free ascent of
Black Fly Festival

Jamie Cunningham

The Wicked Roof (project)
The obvious huge roof at the far end of the Lower Slab. Set up a top rope and give it a go!

Squirrel Meat (a.k.a. Omnivore) 5.10b
Around to the left of the large roof, start into an alcove and step off a pile of broken stones and onto a clean face. Climb past two bolts (crux) and into a large flake above. Follow this with natural gear to the top. 45′
2 bolts, nuts/cams to #2.5
FA: Jon Sykes May, 1999

Bombs Away 5.10a

Climb the overhanging fist crack to the left of Squirrel Meat. Big pro and athletic tape are definitely recommended. For an easier finish, move right below the overhang on a large flake, and finish on Squirrel Meat. Nuts/cams to #4

FA: Kai Poesse and Brian Whitfield August, 1998

★ Rocket 5.10d

Start into the same alcove as Bombs Away and at the start of the overhang, move left up the steep finger crack. Exit with a difficult move at the top and belay from the tree. Nuts/cams to #2

FA: Kai Poesse and Brian Whitfield August, 1998
FFA: Chris Marks and Jon Sykes May, 1999

Middle Ledge

5.9 Project

5.10/5.11 Project

★ Shoot Up or Shut Up 5.10b

Climb delicate moves up a clean face to a single bolt, 15 feet up. Clip the bolt and move into the crack system above. Climb the crack to the top, make the tricky exit move and head for the tree to belay. 60'
1 bolt, nuts/cams to #2.5

FA: Brian Whitfield and Kai Poesse December, 1998

★ Free For All 5.10c

Just to the left of Shoot Up or Shut Up, reach for a single bolt below a small bulge. Pull over the bulge and clip another bolt. Follow the flake and crack system to the right of a large resting boulder and a smooth face. Without stepping off the boulder, climb straight up the face past two more bolts (crux) to the top. Belay at the tree. 60' 4 bolts, nuts/cams to #1

FA: Brian Whitfield and Jon Sykes May, 1999

Brian Whitfield, the leading force behind the development of First Ledge, on the first ascent of Free For All

Jamie Cunningham

First Ledge

Little Feat 5.9+

On the far right hand corner of First Ledge, start at the very bottom of the slab below a bolt (15 feet up). Climb up past down sloping flakes to a small stance below the first bolt. Tiny holds lead up to a small flake (crux), then up easier holds to the second bolt. Run it out on lower angle face for 15 feet, then head up and slightly left over the final bulge on good holds. Belay at the tree on the overlook. 70′ 2 bolts, nuts/cams to #2

FA: Chuck Woodman and Drew Craig June, 1999

★ Hunchback Crack 5.10a

Climb the steep and strenuous finger crack to a horizontal crack. Continue past a bolt to the anchor. 1 bolt, nuts/TCUs
FA: Jon Sykes and Chris Marks May, 1999

Thin Lizzy 5.9+

Just to the left of Hunchback, climb up thin, balance face moves past three bolts to the anchor. Fun, but short. 35' 3 bolts
FA: Brian Whitfield and Kai Poesse August, 1998

Frosted Flake 5.7

Start in the corner of the large diamond shaped flake. Move to the farthest point left, then head right along the flake to the anchor. Rap off or mantle onto the ledge then continue up to the right to finish up on top. A bit of a runout! 60' nuts/cams to #4
FA: Chuck Woodman and Janel McDonald September, 1995

★ Stiff Little Fingers 5.10d/5.11a

Start up the same corner as Frosted Flake, then move left up the overhung face to a bolt. Difficult underclings lead to the magic hold and another bolt (crux). Follow the unrelentingly difficult flake past three more bolts to an anchor. Rap off the route. 70' 5 bolts, nuts/cams to #2
FA: Scott Whitfield May, 1998
FFA: Chris Marks and Jon Sykes May, 1999

Crescent Moon 5.5

Before reaching the base of First Ledge, head left on the trail to the obvious half moon crack. Climb this to the top (unprotected).
FA: Chuck Woodman September, 1999

Green Line 5.6

Just to the left of the previous route, in a left-facing corner is a nice crack in a green mossy face. Ooze up this to the top. Walk off.
FA: Chuck Woodman September, 1995

Upper Cliff

(Routes described from right to left)

Mossy Madness 5.7

Climb up the mossy face on cleaned holds past a series of horizontal cracks and onto a ledge. Climb left up the crack and run it out to the top. 50'
Nuts/cams to #2
FA: Brian Whitfield and Kai Poesse July, 1999

★ Fatty Acid (a.k.a. Second Time's a Winner) 5.9+

Climb the right-slanting seam to a tricky mantle onto the ledge. Then move up the steep headwall past two bolts and run it out to the tree at the top. 50' 2 bolts, nuts/cams to #2
FA: Brian Whitfield and Kai Poesse July, 1999
FFA: Jon Sykes and Brian Whitfield August, 1999

Strange Days 5.6

Move up the large crack and onto the ledge. Stay in the corner and protect in a nice crack before climbing over a tricky block at the top. 50'
Nuts/cams to #3
FA: Brian Whitfield and Kai Poesse June, 1999

★ Amino Maker 5.9+

Just to the left of Strange Days, start at the lowest point on the face. Climb up the face on difficult holds past two bolts. Protect in the downward flakes before moving over a wedged block and into a crack. Follow the crack to the top. 50' 2 bolts, nuts/cams to #3
FA: Brian Whitfield and Kai Poesse June, 1999

Mexican Radio 5.7

Go under the large fallen birch tree to the obvious finger crack. Climb the crack on the right hand side to the ledge. Continue up the cracks and onto some large quartz holds that lead to the top. 70' Nuts/cams to #2
FA: Kai Poesse and Brian Whitfield May, 1999

Free Clinic 5.7

Climb the finger crack on the left to a large block. Continue up left of the small roof on good face moves. Nuts/cams to #2
FA: Kai Poesse and Brian Whitfield May, 1999

Potash Knob

High above the East Branch of the Pemigewasset River, just across from Loon Mountain Ski Area, is a small crag that offers many high-quality routes from 50 to 120 feet long with the potential of yielding even more gems to those who like solitude and don't mind a stiff approach hike. South facing, with great views of the ski area, Scar Ridge and Mt. Osceola, this area is especially appealing in the spring when deep snow still blocks the more sheltered approaches, and in the fall.

One half-mile east of the Loon Mountain Ski Area's entrance, bear left

at a sign which says "Clearbrook." Head up the road for 100 yards, then bear right past many condominiums for about 1/2 mile to the end of the road. Park in any spot marked "V" for visitor and head up into the woods on the right side of the last condo. A rough trail with ribbons leads steeply up past huge boulders to an overgrown talus slope and the left side of the cliff. The cliff consists of a low-angle slab to the left and steep walls and slabs to the right.

The author about to have a daytime nightmare on the first ascent of Daytime Nightmare

Chuck Woodman

Routes are described from left to right. There is potential for boulder development on this approach.

Trick or Treat I 5.6

1. Locate a clean white streak on the far left end of the cliff. Climb the clean streak to a bush, then head up and right to a bolt on a short, steep headwall. Traverse a ramp up and left and finish at a fir tree. 100′

FA: Chuck Woodman October, 1995

Drop Zone I 5.7

The climb is so named because of a large white rock perched precariously at the finish.

Start 50 feet right of the previous route at the lowest part of the slab.

1. Climb the low-angle slab to a small fir on the left, then continue straight up to a steeper 20-foot headwall. Moderate climbing on good rock leads to the trees. 120′

FA: Chuck Woodman October, 1995

100 feet right of the first two climbs, the cliff rears up much more steeply, forming a wall about 60 to 100 feet high. The next climbs are found here. From the top of the trail, scramble up a broken area for 30 feet, then walk right.

★ Battle of the Bulge I 5.10b

1. Climb up a slab, place a medium cam in a slot, then move up and right with difficulty to the first bolt. Continue up left along a narrow ledge past more bolts, then surmount the final bulge using the hidden holds on perfect rock. Finish straight up a slightly runout slab, and reach the trees. 60′

FA: Chuck Woodman and Ken Parker November, 1995

End of the Line I 5.9

1. Ten feet right of Battle of the Bulge, climb up flakes past two bolts and make a tricky mantle to a good ledge. Boulder up past one more bolt (crux), pass a wide crack on the left (good large cam here) and reach a large fir tree. 60′

FA: Chuck Woodman and Ken Parker November, 1995

★ Nose Dive I 5.10c

Moving 10 feet right of End of the Line, locate a line of bolts just to the left of a large, broken chimney.

1. Climb up right slanting grooves with increasing difficulty past two bolts, (crux), then swing up over a bulge to another bolt and the end of the difficulties. Continue on lower-angled slabs to a steeper headwall (5.9, easier on right) and an awkward finish up a slightly rotten corner. 100'

History: The climb received its name when just as the leader was making the crux moves past the second bolt, a loose hold ripped off, sending him plummeting earthward. An alert Ken Parker yarded in the rope, preventing the leader from hitting the jagged rocks of the chimney.

FA: Chuck Woodman and Ken Parker November, 1995

The following climbs are accessed by climbing back down the 30-foot broken area, then walking east along the bottom of the cliff, which is mainly a steep wall covered with moss and lichen. After about 80 feet, you come to a large rock next to a tree growing close to the wall.

Wings of Stone II 5.11a AO

1. Climb a cleaned strip of smooth rock past a bolt (5.10a), step left and fight up a surprisingly awkward wide crack to a bush and a belay at a small fir tree. 50'

2. Scramble up easy rock for 10 feet, then make a scary step across a yawning crevice and clip a bolt. Easy aid or extremely difficult free climbing leads up past two more bolts. Beyond the last bolt, struggle past an enormous raven's nest on a large ledge, then climb a sharp, but dirty crack to a large tree on the left. 60'

FA: Chuck Woodman and Ken Parker November, 1995

Continuing along the cliff bottom about 150 feet beyond the start of the previous climb, scramble first right, then left, up past a large uprooted tree and reach a sloping tree-covered ledge. Following this ledge left will take you all the way back to the start of the second pitch of Wings of Stone. Head up and right to reach a steep wall with a huge roof at its right end.

Fall From Grace I 5.10c

1. Scramble up broken ledges to reach a bolt, then climb straight up through a small overhanging corner to another bolt. Head up and right with little pro (small Lowe Ball) to reach a stance and crack. An awkward mantle leads to a good ledge on the left. A bolt protects very thin moves up a slab. Belay after 15 feet at a small fir. 70'

FA: Chuck Woodman and Kai Poesse November, 1998

Daytime Nightmare I 5.6 A4+

The huge roof on the right side of the upper wall does have a route through it. A lone bolt marks the start on a slab below the roof.

1. Free-climb past the bolt to a horizontal crack. Step right to the start of a crack/seam shooting out the roof. Nail this to the edge (A3) and a poorly placed rivet. Bat hook up the blank vertical wall (A4+) to the top.

FA: Jon Sykes and Chuck Woodman May 13,1999

Route listings for Potash Knob (see topos next page)

1. Trick Or Treat 5.6
2. Drop Zone 5.7
3. Battle of the Bulge 5.10b
4. End of the Line 5.9
5. Nose Dive 5.10c
6. Wings of Stone II 5.11a A0
7. Fall From Grace 5.10c
8. Project
9. Project
10. Project
11. Project
12. Daytime Nightmare 5.6 A4+

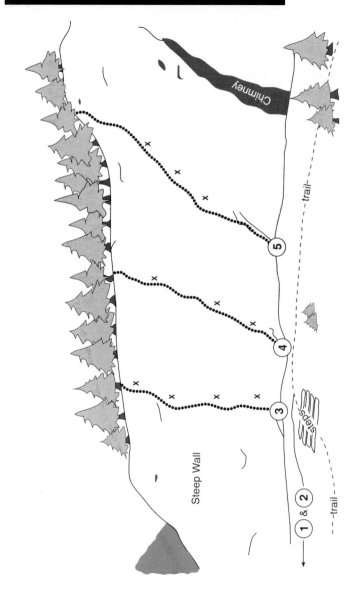

Potash Knob left side

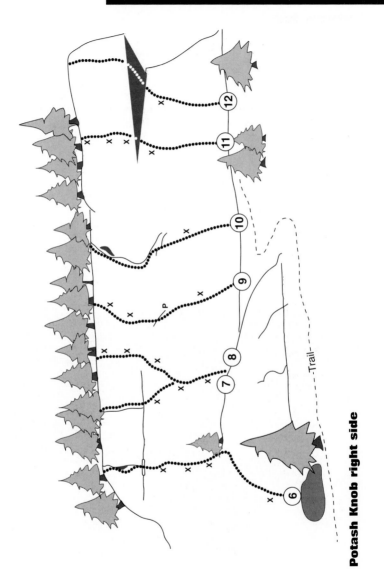

Potash Knob right side

Cannon Ice

More than any place else in the east, climbing Cannon in the winter, whether it be on ice or rock, requires total commitment from you, the climber.

The cliff is not for beginners learning to climb, nor for the intermediate climber picking off his or her tick list of must-do climbs. Cannon is for seasoned veterans with years of experience in many different facets of winter climbing. You must put in your time climbing the hard routes elsewhere before you step foot on Cannon.

The average weather in winter in the Notch is windy, cold, and snowy. Sunny days are rare, and a no wind day is unheard of. Always climb with an experienced leader who has been on Cannon many times, or hire a guide the first time, because your life depends on it.

Why do I make this sound so intense? Because Cannon represents the ultimate in challenge and commitment in the eastern United States. Its routes hold the potential for some of the greatest climbing rewards and failures. Climb smart and live long. Routes are described from left to right (south to north).

Cannon Cliff in winter   Jamie Cunningham

La Deepfreeze III NEI 2-4

This is no longer a short route. Several pitches can be climbed using the original start, but finishing on short vertical flows near the top adds to the length and difficulty of the climb. Start the climb about 100 feet south of the Henderson Buttress at a mixed gully. Ascend the gully 200 feet to a tree ledge and rappel or continue in any direction above, heading toward a couple of vertical flows and the top.

FA: Todd Swain and Brad White January 17, 1981

Henderson II 5.5

A loose, snow-packed rock climb, safer in winter than in the summer.

FWA: Ajax Greene and Rick Mulhern 1974

★ Omega IV NEI 5+

Omega is considered by many to be the single greatest climbing goal in New Hampshire in winter. After 25 years and many advances in technology, Omega is still a very committing and dangerous ice climb. It is located several hundred yards left (south) of the Whitney-Gilman ridge, just left of a smaller buttress. The larger Muir buttress stands between Whitney-Gilman Ridge and the smaller buttress.

Omega is three pitches long with the first pitch having three variations. The most direct start is thinly verglassed with very little protection. A variation starts 20 feet right in a steep broken corner and

The classic Omega in typical thin conditions
Jamie Cunningham

lands you on top of the smaller buttress. Alternatively, you can climb the buttress on its right side at 5.6 up to a rusty pin belay 30 feet right of the second pitch. The second pitch—the crux—involves thin ice, little protection, and a hanging curtain of ice. The last pitch is steep ice with the best protection of the climb. At the top, walk up and left to connect with the Whitney-Gilman descent trail.

FA: John Bouchard and Rainsford Rouner February, 1976

Local Jim Shimberg soloed Omega in late March, 2000. This is the hardest solo to date in the White Mountains.

Aboriginal Rhythmic Implement NEI 3+ 5.9 A1 (a.k.a. Tom Tom)

More of a winter rock climb or mixed climb than an ice route. Be prepared to do lots of dry tooling. Bring nuts and cams to 4" and a good selection of thin pins. Start on the buttress 75' down and right of the start of Omega. Rope up at a birch tree.

1. Climb a crack to gain the ridge. Climb the ridge and belay at a birch tree. 150'
2. Climb up and right across a snowfield to a left-facing corner, which leads to a good ledge. Continue up another left-facing corner to another ledge with a fixed anchor. 120'
3. Climb up a V-groove to a good ledge. Climb the corner above to a stance, then follow the flake left to a ledge. Climb the crack to a ledge with small trees. Traverse right 50' across this ledge to a belay. 130'
4. The exact line above this belay will vary according to conditions. Step left and climb on top of a block (pin). Use three points of aid, one fixed, to gain a crack arching right to a belay. 60'
5. Traverse right into a gully with small trees. Step left, and climb a small snowfield, then climb straight up on difficult mixed ground, finishing in a right-facing corner with thick ice. 165'

Comment: This climb can be done in a variety of conditions, from thick ice to bare rock. No need to wait for it to come into shape.

FA: Tom Nonnis and Tom Callaghan March 20, 2000

★ The Whitney-Gilman Ridge III 5.7

This the best winter rock climb on Cannon. In mountain boots, it offers you many obstacles to overcome. Rock shoes are recommended for speed. See page 39 for the route description.

FWA: Leif Patterson and Henry W. Kendall 1962

Across the Great Divide IV 5.7 A4

This climb ascends the overhung north wall just right of the Whitney-Gilman Ridge. The first ascent was done over several days in full winter conditions.

FA: Peter Cole and Rick Wilcox climbed pitch one, then Cole, Mark Richey, and Rainsford Rouner did the second pitch. Peter Cole and Rick Wilcox finally finished the climb in November, 1975

★ The Black Dike IV NEI 4+/5-

More than any other route in the White Mountains, the Dike represents a stepping stone for many aspiring ice climbers. Since its first ascent, solo on December 18, 1971, by young and brash John Bouchard, the Dike has become one of the most sought after ice climbs in the east. Unfortunately, it has also become one of the most crowded routes.

Due to the crowding and the inherent nature of the Dike, a warning to all those attempting this route is necessary. The Black Dike is a challenging climb in and of itself, but can also become extremely dangerous if there are too many climbers attempting to ascend at the same time. Climbing below other climbers on this route is hazardous. The Dike acts as a funnel for any ice that falls from above and therefore even two parties climbing at once are too many.

Henry Barber on the second ascent of The Black Dike   Rick Wilcox

One problem that seems to occur is that climbers traveling through the area who are pressed for time ignore basic climbing logic and push ahead in their pursuit of bagging this route regardless of the traffic on the Dike. Choosing to climb behind others could very well be the undoing of many an aspiring climber, be it on the Dike or any other ice climb. This warning is offered for the safety of all climbers unfamiliar with the Dike.

Hike up and right of Whitney-Gilman Ridge into the immense dark gully. Climb low-angled rock and ice with very little protection up to and slightly right of the main gully to a belay stance below a smaller, pronounced rock face. The crux pitch climbs the notorious hard-to-protect rock traverse heading left into the main gully. Alternatively, you can step down and left and climb a narrow ice runnel that forms in the gully. Both variations lead to an old pin belay in fractured rock. Back this belay up with an ice belay. The last pitch follows bulges up past several stances to a point at which you can climb either the longer left side, or climb up and

right and into the woods. To descend, follow a marked trail uphill for a hundred yards then left and down through the woods on an extremely steep path; care is needed in early season because the trail is very icy.
FA: John Bouchard
December 18, 1971

Brian Whitfield nears
the top of the second
pitch of the Black Dike

Jamie Cunningham

Variation: Hassig's Direct NEI 5

Ascend mixed rock and ice directly above the first belay on the Black Dike and at its top, traverse back left to the second belay, or head straight up to the top.

FA: Chris Hassig February, 1979

★ Fafnir IV NEI 5

The next obvious flow is to the right (north) of the Black Dike and follows a series of steep steps. Climb the first pitch of the Dike, then from the belay step right and follow steep bulges of ice up to a good snow ledge. The last pitch (the crux) follows more steep bulges up to a mixed finish off right, or you can climb straight up exiting left on more difficult ground. Conditions vary from day to day.

FA: John Bouchard, Steve Zajchowski, and Roger Martin December, 1975
A full-length ice route between Fafnir and Lila was climbed by John Bouchard and friend around 1997/98. No other information is known.

★ Lila IV NEI 4+ M6

This is the first route on Cannon given the mixed rating. Tom Nonnis and John Courtney dry-tooled the A2 section in the winter of 1999, opening the door for future climbers to push the limits in the mixed realm. Climb the verglassed slab just left of the Cannonade Buttress for a full pitch. Thicker ice leads you to a rock headwall and a vertical crack system which you dry tool up to loose blocky climbing and the top.

FA: Rainsford Rouner and Nancy Kerrebrock March, 1976
FFA: Tom Nonnis and John Courtney February, 1999
History note: Around 1987, Tom Nonnis soloed the first ascent of several ice routes across the notch near the Eaglet and Eagle Cliff, notably Late Night With Yellow Toe.

Cannonade II NEI 2-3 5.4

Basic mixed climbing with loose rock and route finding. Rarely climbed.
FWA: Robert Hall, Jorge Uriosite, and Joe Boden 1967

★ Quartet Ice Hose IV NEI 4+ 5.8

Like Omega, Quartet rarely comes into shape. It was finally climbed to the top in one day by Jim Shimberg and Mark Davis in the winter of 1998. Many strong parties, including John Bouchard and Jim Donini, attempted

A young John Bragg, one of the leading forces of winter ascents on Cannon in the '70s, enjoying a wonderful day in the Notch

Rick Wilcox

the route, yet a local succeeded. The first two pitches were first climbed by Peter Cole. Then in January 1981, Ed Webster and Todd Swain made a nearly complete ascent, bailing out near the top in the dark. Chris Dube and Larry Sodano made the first continuous ascent on December 9 and 10, 1989. Just left of Duet Direct is the Quartet Corner with an ice runnel deep in the cleft. The first pitch is always thin with very little protection. The second pitch climbs the runnel up to the top of Duet Buttress. From there the possibilities are endless. Follow the easiest line to the top.

Duet III 5.7

It took just six speedy hours in snowy conditions for the first winter ascent.

FWA: Andy Tuthill and Chris Ellms 1977

Rodan (Icarus) IV 5.11b

(The first new route to be climbed on Cannon in the winter.) John Bouchard and Rick Wilcox, with help from Jeff Pheasant, completed the route with one bivouac in January of 1974. For added adventure, Bouchard broke his ankle near the top. The original A4 was never found on the first free ascent in September of 1989. The route starts on the right (north) side of the Duet Buttress and follows steep corners right of Raven Crack eventually connecting with the upper pitches of Duet.

★ Sam's Swan Song   III 5.7

A bold and impressive winter ascent for that time.
FWA: Robert Proudman and Mark Lawrence over two days in 1967.

★ The Ghost   IV 5.7 A3

With time and advances in technology this route almost can be enjoyed in winter. The first winter ascent of the Ghost was a bold, cold bit of climbing over two days in 1973 by John Bouchard, Rick Wilcox, and Henry Barber.

★ VMC Direct Direct   IV 5.10+ (5.9 C2)

The first winter ascent of this classic route fell to a multi-national team that took four days and one bivouac in hammocks to complete the climb.
FWA: John Bouchard, Jeff Pheasant, David Beldon (France), and Jean-Claude Droyer (France) in 1975.

★ Labyrinth Wall
V 5.7 A4

Rainsford Rouner and Peter Cole completed the first winter ascent in warm weather with one bivouac in February of 1976.
FWA: Rainsford Rouner and Peter Cole February, 1976

John Bouchard on the
first ascent of Icarus

Rick Wilcox

★ Fruit Cup Wall   V 5.8 A4

In 1975, while still in high school, a young Mark Richey rope-soloed all but the last pitch in a bold attempt for the first winter ascent. It was finally climbed to the top with one bivouac by a three-man team in 1978.
FWA: Mark Whiton, Bryan Becker, and Alain Comeau

★ Moby Grape   III 5.8

One of the best 5.8 free climbs, done in rapid time.
FWA: Andy Tuthill and Chris Ellms February, 1976

★ Union Jack   III 5.9

Enjoyable in summer, but in winter with mountain boots on, it becomes much more difficult. Wait for a warmer day and wear rock climbing shoes for maximum control.
FWA: Chris Hassig and friend 1978

★ Vertigo   III 5.9 A0

The first winter ascent of this summer classic took two days using wire nuts (stoppers) for protection and very little direct aid.
FWA: Chris Hassig and Dave Foster 1976

North-South-West   III 5.9

In winter, this wandering route, with ice and snow on its many faces, can be an extremely arduous undertaking.
FWA: Chris Ellms and Andy Tuthill 1976

Old Cannon   III 5.6

The best and safest time to climb Old Cannon is in the winter when most of the loose blocks are frozen in place.
FWA: Robert Hall and Jorge Uriosite 1971

★ Unnamed   III NEI 3+/4+

This seldom-formed, full-length route saw its first complete ascent by John Bouchard and Mark Richey in 1997. It takes a fairly direct line starting at the corner at the base of Wiessner's Buttress, which leads to the Old Cannon Garden. First climbed by Andy Tuthill and Jim Rossin in 1976.

From the Garden, follow more difficult mixed ground between Whale Watcher, on your left, and Riddler, on your right. This will bring you to the top above the Old Man's Head. Ratings will vary dramatically from year to year so be prepared for anything.

One other route was climbed by John Bouchard and Mark Richey left of the unnamed route (previous page) around the same time, in the winter of 1997. No other information is known. Both routes form only after heavy rain and a flash freeze.

★ Wiessner's Buttress III 5.6

Like many old routes on Cannon, once it's frozen in place, it becomes safer to climb. This is a worthwhile mixed route at a moderate grade.
FWA: Joe Cote and Steve Arenault 1971

★ Lakeview II NEI 2 5.5

On the first winter ascent the entire slabs were coated in ice and snow. A fun challenge in mountain boots as a pure winter rock climb.
FWA: Tom Lyman, Rick Wilcox, and A.J. Lafleur Winter 1969

★ Adam's Slide II NEI 2

This is one of the oldest winter climbs in the eastern United States. Although mostly a snow climb, it was a bold ascent in 1919 by Dartmouth Outing Club (D.O.C) members. Former governor Sherman Adams, who was considered by the D.O.C. to be too independent, led his team up the obvious steep snow and ice slope just right of the Lakeview Slabs landing them on the Lunch Ledge below the Old Man's Head.
FA: Sherman Adams, Ellis Griggs, and D.W. Trainer March 3, 1919

Echo Crag Ice Climbing

When conditions are in, Echo Crag has an incredible variety of moderate to hard ice and mixed climbs. With routes like Hollow Hell, Scottish Gully, and Spirit Within, and desperates such as Final Confrontation, the Hermit, the wild Toothless Wonder with its exposed finish, and the stinger pillar of Fear of the Unknown, there is definitely diverse fun for many to enjoy. Its downside is that its ice forms and falls off quickly due to sun exposure during the afternoon. If conditions are fat elsewhere, Echo ice will be in. Routes are described from left to right (north to south) as one approaches the cliff from the trail. All routes on Echo Crag are Grade I.

Please be advised that almost all winter routes at Echo Crag are summer rock climbs. The use of pitons should be kept to a minimum. Also, care should be taken while using crampons and ice axes—misuse of these can scar the rock. If you are incapable of ascending a route without skidding and scraping the rocks, then do not attempt to climb it until you have attained more skill.

Square Inch Wall

Rock A Bye Billy Boy NEI 3+
This is a seldom-formed runnel of ice 20 feet left of Hollow Hell. Climb a shallow right-facing corner up to and past a short, steep face to the top. 35'
FA: Jon Sykes and Bill Rzepa December 11, 1996

★ Hollow Hell NEI 4
Hollow columns require rock gear for pro, with lots of hooking up this beauty. Another flow forms just to the right on occasion. 40'
FA: Jon Sykes, Rope-solo January, 1994

Side Stepping the Issue NEI 3+ 5.6
Just right of Hollow Hell is an ice-covered blocky slab leading to a steep face 15 feet up. At base of steep face traverse right with hands in horizontal crack until you come to a corner, (right-facing) mixed climb to top. 60'
FA: Jon Sykes and Brian Chartier February, 1995

★ Mack Jam NEI 4
Climb detached columns through an overlap to steep sustained climbing above. A hard forty-footer.
FWA: Chris Marks and Jon Sykes January 29, 1998

Art Mooney leads the short, but steep, Hollow Hell
Eric Pospesil

One Swing Away NEI 3+

Avalanche summer route. A rare thin drip that sometimes forms late season to make this a commanding lead. Good rock pro. At first set of stairs climb drip direct to top. Tree rappel. 60'
FA: Jon Sykes, Rope-solo March, 1994

Threading The Alpine Needle NEI 2+ 5.5

Starts at the top of first stairs. Climb up easy gully and follow wide crack to ledge and white birch tree. Above finish up a crack 5.5 through the center of the top overlap. 60'
FA: Jon Sykes, Rope-solo January, 1994

Moments after this shot was taken, the author was spit off the thin ice above sustaining a pulled back. You can't climb everything...

Jamie Cunningham

Justin Melnick leads a
"fat" Scottish Gully

Jon Sykes

Tardy But Still First NEI 3 5.6

A rare mixed route forms on Skeletal Ribs (summer route), offering good protection and interesting, fun climbing.

FA: Gareth Slattery, Mike Lee, and Jamie Cunningham January 30, 1999

★ Scottish Gully NEI 3+ 5.4

Climb iced gully to small stance, then up thicker ice for thirty more feet to rock climbing above. 60'

FWA: Jon Sykes, Rope-solo December, 1993

The author seeks guidance from the feisty ferret on Ferret Legger's first ascent
Jamie Cunningham

Ferrett Legger NEI 3+ 5.6
Wafer-thin, bolt-protected slab with a vertical crack finish.
FA: Jon Sykes, Chris Marks, and Gareth Stattery December, 1996

Sackless NEI 3 5.7
Just past Cinch Sack is a right-facing corner leading to a rounded vertical crack system to the top. 60'
FWA: Jon Sykes, Rope-solo Winter, 1994

Chris Marks bulls through the crux of Lip Service

Eric Pospesil

The Shield

★ Spirit Within NEI 4 5.7

Climb thin ice on the face just right of the gully past trees to a large ledge 40 feet up. One can climb the gully as well. You are now under a large roof system. Step right on ledge to a left-facing corner, climb it to a stance just right of roofs, clip bolt to a summer rock route (Ed's Weed Be Gone), and traverse right on a four- to six-inch ledge past another bolt on another rock route (Wesley's Aspiration); hard clip. Traverse right until you reach steep ice leading to the top. 120'

FA: Jon Sykes January, 1994

The author experimenting on the first winter ascent of Social Experiment
Jamie Cunningham

★ Lip Service   NEI 4 M7

The newest addition to Echo Crag, Lip Service has been attempted several times over the past few years. Chris Marks, with encouragement from Team Bubba, finally pieced the puzzle together, creating the hardest mixed route to date in Franconia Notch.

Start at the Spirit Within gully, and, at the top of the gully, move up under the main roof and make a hard move to clip a bolt on an unnamed 5.10b rock route. With your remaining strength, pull through the hanging curtain and reach the top.

FA: Chris Marks, Art Mooney, Jon Sykes, and Peter Ducette   Dec., 2000

★ Ed's Weed Be Gone to Spirit Within   NEI 4 5.6

Climb vertical crack on Ed's and finish on Spirit Within.
FA: Jon Sykes and Mike Lee   December 10, 1996

★ Wesley's Aspiration   NEI 4+

Very thin technical ice and marginal pro make this a bold run for your money. Climb a runnel of ice up to a horizontal break, follow small

columns (delicate) to an arch, then step right and climb final ribbons of ice to top and trees. 70′
FWA: Jon Sykes and Chris Marks January 29, 1996

★ Crucial Evidence   NEI 4

Look for a lone bolt on a slab. Tiptoe up 1/2-inch ice past bolt to horizontal crack and detached columns over an overlap. Pull over this (crux) to mixed climbing and the top. 70′
FWA: Jon Sykes and Chuck Woodman February 20, 1996

★ Social Experiment   NEI 4+

Ten feet right of Crucial Evidence is the steeper and harder sister climb. A lone bolt protects the face start, then natural gear through two overlaps and face above. Rappel from trees. 70′
FWA: Jon Sykes and Jamie Cunningham January 30, 1999

★ The Shield   NEI 3+ 5.7

A ribbon of ice forms down this face occasionally. From a stance on top of two flakes, move up a 20-foot high buttress to a ledge below an overlap. Now step over the left side of overlap into a thin vertical crack which splits the upper face. A final, small overlap leads to the top. 75′
FWA: Jon Sykes, Rope-solo January, 1994

The Grunge Wall

★ Vaporub   NEI 3

This is the obvious, bushy ledge (stairway) system that separates the Shield from the Grunge Wall. Climb up thin to thicker ice ribbon with some rock protection to trees. 75′
FA: Jon Sykes and Lois LaRock January 22, 1996

★ Carpet Path   NEI 3+ 5.6

With good rock gear, the thin ice on this seldom-formed route makes this a real gem. Twenty feet right of Vaporub is a face with good horizontal edges/cracks throughout the climb. Ascend rock and ice straight up face to two-bolt belay. 75′
FWA: Jon Sykes, Rope-solo December, 1993

★ Swing Easy, Climb Hard NEI 3+ 5.6 R

Fifteen feet right of Carpet Path is a mini-buttress with a left-facing inside corner. Start here with mixed climbing up this buttress to a stance, then step back right and up thin minimally-protected ice to fatter more protectable ice and the top. This climb forms every year and varies in condition. 75'

FA: Jon Sykes, Rope-solo December, 1993

Sleep in the Dry Spot NEI 3+ 5.6

FWA: Chris Marks Winter, 1996

★ Alpine Grunge NEI 3+

Begin 30 feet to the right of Swing Easy/Climb Hard. Climb a small rib of ice, head straight for the top. 60'
FA: Jon Sykes and Chris Marks January, 1995

Amphitheater Ice NEI 2 to 3+

Great practice area for first-timers. 40 to 60 feet.
FA: unknown

Mike Lee enjoying "fat" ice on Alpine Grunge

Jon Sykes

Bill Keiler seconding
the first ascent of
Syko's Pillars

Jon Sykes

The Hermit Haven

Hell Bent on Birch NEI 3+

Starting 10 feet left (north) of Syko's Pillars, climb the steep face up to a hanging birch at the top. 40'
FA: Jon Sykes and Chris Kratt March 13, 1998

★ Syko's Pillars NEI 4+

Twenty feet left of Patella Swella Corner are two side-by-side free-standing pillars. Pins and natural pro are recommended. 50'
FA: Jon Sykes and Bill Keiler March 7, 1996

Chris Marks scratching
out the first ascent of
Patella Swella

Jon Sykes

★ Psychotic Satisfaction (Direct Finish) NEI 4

This is the direct finish up a free-hanging pillar instead of the wandering
line of Psychotic Reaction. There is also a bold direct start below the direct
finish done by Chris Marks and Justin Melnick in the winter of 1999. 40'
(See route info for start just below.)
FA: Jon Sykes March 13, 1998

Psychotic Reaction NEI 4 5.6 R

Ten feet right of Syko's Pillars is a rock step to a corner leading up to a large
ledge. Climb up to the ledge, step right past a pin to a right-facing corner
(Patella Swella). Work your way up the corner ten feet, step right again into
another right-facing corner and climb this to the top and the trees. 90'
FA: Jon Sykes and Tim Kemple, Sr. December, 1994

★ Patella Swella   NEI 3+/4

Follow the right-facing corner with thin pro and thinner ice to top. 60'
FA: Chris Marks and Jon Sykes February, 1995

★ Spanking Bilbo   NEI 4+

Five feet right of Patella Swella corner is a very steep thin runnel of ice going straight up. Mixed free moves at the start. 60'
FA: Jon Sykes and Bill Keiler March 7, 1996
FFA: Jon Sykes January 22, 1998

★ Final Confrontation   NEI 4+

Climb a slightly overhung pillar system just five feet right of Spanking Bilbo. Very hard. 60'
FA: Jon Sykes and Chuck Woodman February 20, 1996

★ The Hermit   NEI 4+

Rarely does this climb form fat ice. Delicate columns down low lead to fatter ice and the top. 60'
FA: Jon Sykes and Chris Kratt March 13, 1998

Eye Opener   NEI 5

This is a variation just right of the Hermit's second pillar. Rare to see it form in its original condition.
FA: Will Gadd and Chris Marks February 22, 1998

The author on an early attempt of The Hermit

Bill Keiler

The Hone Wall

Alpine Diddy NEI 3+

Climb the mixed rock and ice ramp up and left to the upper wall and steeper more sustained ice. Many variations above. 100'

FA: Jon Sykes, Rope-solo January, 1994

Thinsicle NEI 3+ R

Ten feet right of Alpine Diddy is a runnel that offers a vertical dance up thin to thicker ice with little protection to help the nerves. 50'

FA: Jon Sykes, Rope-solo December, 1994

Thank God for Turf NEI 3 5.6

Ten feet right of Thinsicle is a stepped wall leading to turf and more rock and ice above. Mixed climbing and tricky pro makes you earn this seldom-formed route. 70'

FA: Jon Sykes, Rope solo December, 1994

★ Toothless Wonder NEI 4 5.7 R

This is one of the bolder routes at Echo.
Climb the steep, iced-up ramp system leading

The author keeps his composure in the tight confines of the upper gully of Toothless Wonder

Jamie Cunningham

to a prominent gully sixty feet up. There is a column of ice flowing out of the gully five feet long and one-foot thick. Tiptoe up this entering into the gully. The climbing in the gully is awkward and scary with minimal pro. A selection of pins is wise. 90′

FA: Jon Sykes and Bill Keiler February 5, 1996
History: Bill Keiler broke a tooth rappelling the route, hence the name.

★ God, I Love This NEI 4

Same start as for Toothless Wonder. Start up ramp until you come to first columns, climb these to stance and step left to more columns. These columns are much more delicate, and hard to protect. Tiptoe your way up these detached columns for forty feet until the angle pitches back some (thin), then follow this to one more column and the top. Rap from bolts. 80′

FWA: Jon Sykes and Chris Marks January 28, 1996

★ Hurry up I'm Hungry NEI 4

Same start as for Toothless Wonder. Climb up ramp to the first columns and follow columns straight up through roof. One more column leads to the top, then rap off bolts. 80′
FWA: Jon Sykes and Chris Marks January 28, 1996

Pat Hacket nabbing the second winter ascent of Hurry Up, I'm Hungry

Jon Sykes

Prayer Girth NEI 4R

Starts just right of a big pine tree on a ledge. Climb thin to thicker ice for 60 feet until under a small overlap. Step left eight feet and surmount thin ice once again until under the final twenty-foot columns. Chug to top and trees. 90′

FA: Jon Sykes and Bill Keiler January 30, 1996

★ Bonsai Gully NEI 4 R

Some thirty feet right of the pine tree is a runnel of ice that will humble even the hardest of the hard core. If you're lucky you'll even find two bolts from a summer rock route to clip (Ants in Your Lycra). Climb the runnel for sixty feet, past the two bolts until under the roof. Clip one more bolt

(The Big Tweek) with a long sling and step left ten feet to start of the gully. Climb up the gully ten feet and step right onto a curtain of ice and climb it to the top and trees. 90′

FA: Jon Sykes, Bill Keiler, and Chris Kratt February 7, 1997

Chris Marks searching his soul and the wafer thin ice of Bonsai Gully

Sykes Collection

★ Fear of the Unknown NEI 4 R

Same start as for Bonsai Gully; climb thin runnel for sixty feet to just under a roof. A ten-foot column of ice forms off the roof and barely touches down to create a very sustained climb from start to finish. 90'
FA: Jon Sykes and Bill Keiler January 30, 1996

★ Sweet Secrets NEI 3+ 5.6

To the right of Fear of the Unknown is a small buttress—the climb starts at the bottom of it. Climb up face with horizontal ledges and thin ice (rock pro), to a ledge with trees, forty feet up. A flow forms on the upper wall that is very enjoyable to climb. Rap from trees.
FA: Jon Sykes and Bill Keiler January, 1996

Bill Keiler follows the first ascent of Fear Of The Unknown   Jon Sykes

Dreamwall

★ The Arete   NEI 3+ 5.8

This is the prominent rounded arete on the left side of the Dreamwall.
Climb arete to top and two-bolt belay on left side of arete. 120′
FWA: Jon Sykes and Becky Smith March, 1994

Profile Cliff

To date, one mixed climb has been done here. See rock description on page
157.

Aztec Warrior   II NEI 3+ 5.6

Access Profile Cliff via Echo Crag Trail. Turn left following the summer
trail to Profile Cliff just before the start of Echo Crag. Climb to the start of
the ice and finish on an exposed dome at 5.6. 130′
FWA: Jon Sykes, Rope-solo February, 1997

Hound's Hump Ridge in winter showing Flu Shot on the left and Late Night
With Yellow Toe in the center.   Jamie Cunningham

Hound's Hump Ridge

Eagle Crag Left

Flushot II NEI 4

To the left of the Eaglet Spire is a system of walls with one noteworthy climb, which can be seen from the Cannon Tram parking lot. Hike from the parking lot to the ice flow by walking a straight line into base of slabs and follow the trees separating the slabs until you are below the climb. Vertical columns hang in space, attainable only by climbing a mushroomed stalagmite thirty feet to its top; continue by stemming against thin vertical ice to a small stance and the final curtain of ice. Rap from trees. 80'
FA: Jon Sykes and Bill Keiler March 3, 1996

Digging to China II NEI 3 5.6 R

Just to the left of the Flatiron is an indistinct gully named China Gully. In the summer, rock and debris constantly tumble down the gully, but in winter it freezes to create a wonderful alpine climb. Approach via the Eaglet Trail.

1. Wade through (usually) chest-deep snow to a birch tree and belay here. From the tree, step right onto a rock buttress and climb steep rock, turf and occasional ice patches to a tree belay. 100'

2. Move left up a steep ramp, then straight up steep ground until you reach trees near the top. Rappel from trees back down the gully. 100'

History: Jon Sykes and Mike Lee completed the ascent on January 10, 2001. An old, soft iron piton was found on the first pitch.

Eagle Crag Center

Garcia-Vega II NEI 4

Looking from the highway up at the Eaglet you will see an ice flow to the right (south) of the spire a few hundred feet in a left-facing corner. Garcia-Vega starts here. Approach via the Eaglet trail and hike up past the Eaglet to the scree gully and head right to the start of the climb. This is a rarely formed route that has stood the test of time.

1. Ascend delicate, thin, unprotected ice (crux) up a steep face and belay just left of the dihedral. 80'

2. Step right and climb the chimney up to and over a chockstone, then up

---

Hound's Hump Ridge & Eagle Crag ice climbing routes

1. Digging To China NEI 3 5.6
2. Garcia Vega showing right and left variations
3. Soiled But Not Foiled

A typical Garcia-Vega in thin conditions. The chimney on the right side was climbed in 1993 by Alan and Skeeder Cattabriga and named Soiled But Not Foiled. There is also a left-hand variation via dry-tooling that connects to a ramp 50' up.

Chris Marks

lower-angle ice to the woods. 140'

To descend, hike up and left through the woods to the top of the scree gully. Descend the gully and head back down on the Eaglet Trail.

FA: Rainsford Rouner, Michael Hartrich, and Peter Cole January, 1975

Hike up to the right side of the Eaglet to a wall up and right of prominent gully. Follow the wall south past Garcia-Vega and down around buttress, up again, and hike up into a hidden amphitheater, with a few possible ice routes. In the middle of this amphitheater lies the main objective, a narrow chimney/dike with ice over one hundred feet long.

Gravitational Pull NEI 4 Mixed

Climb very thin ice on a steep slab with some stemming for twenty feet until you come to a hanging curtain of ice flowing off an overlap. Natural gear and pins are recommended throughout the climb. Hook tools into curtain, and pull up to more secure ice. Climb a thin, but fun gully to trees

and rap with two ropes. 140'
FA: Jon Sykes and Gareth Slattery December 2, 1995

A third class hike south up along broken walls brings one to a wonderful ice climb in a dramatic setting.

★ Late Night with Yellow Toe   II NEI 3+

Climb stepped gully with mixed pro to a lone hemlock. Rap from tree with two ropes. 130'
FRA: Jon Sykes and Gareth Slattery December 3, 1995
This route was soloed by Tom Nonnis in 1987/88 along with other climbs in this area.
History: Gareth followed the route in darkness and all that could be seen was the yellow toes of his plastic boots.

The author topping out after sustaining a broken nose from an ice fall on Garcia-Vega

Chris Marks

Access to these next five climbs is via the small slide down and to the left of Eagle Cliff. Ascend the slide until you meet a headwall, then traverse right a couple hundred feet to the climbs. There is an ice flow that starts at this headwall and follows an easy cleft for four pitches of fun grade II ice. First ascent unknown.

Heightened Awareness   II NEI 3+

This is the first climb you come to from the slide. A thin start can be avoided via a ramp on the right. Protection is found at the base of the final columns. 80'

FA: Jon Sykes, Gareth Slattery, and Mike Lee January 1, 1997

★ Burn Station   II NEI 3   5.6

Thirty feet right of Heightened Awareness is an open amphitheater. Take the line of least resistance to the trees. 180'

FA: Jon Sykes and Steve Dupuis February 1, 1998

★ Resolution Gully   II NEI 3+

This is a classic alpine route with grand views of Franconia Notch and fun, interesting climbing on a one-pitch flow. One hundred feet right of Heightened Awareness is a beautiful open gully with two starts. The right-hand start is unprotected for thirty feet. The left side has just a ten-foot, unprotected, thin start. The left side is the gully proper and the better of the two starts. Rap from trees at top. 150'

FA: Gareth Slattery, Jon Sykes, and Mike Lee January 1, 1997
Left Start: Jon Sykes and Steve Dupuis February 1, 1998

★ A Slice of Meat in a Rock Sandwich   II NEI 4 R Mixed

This is one of the most interesting climbs in Franconia Notch. Thirty feet right of Resolution Gully is a hidden cleft. An ice runnel forms on the right wall and leads to a mini amphitheater with one more wall with mixed climbing. Rap from trees at Resolution Gully. 130'

FA: Jon Sykes and Mike Lee January 8, 1997

The author on an early attempt of Slice Of Meat In A Rock Sandwich

Mike Lee

Eagle Cliff

One lone ice climb exists on Eagle Cliff, on the far left side. Access Eagle Cliff via Greenleaf Trail to Eagle Pass. Look for trail on left. If you come to the pass, you have gone too far.

Eagle Vision II NEI 4 5.5 R

Climb a blocky, loose rock gully on the left side of the cliff for 100 feet until you reach the base of a 50-foot pillar. Ascend the pillar to its top. There is a bolt and fixed wire nut for rappeling. 150′

FA: Jon Sykes and Bill Keiler January 31, 1996

The author leads the first ascent of Eagle Vision on Eagle Cliff   Mike Lee

Ace of Spades Amphitheater

Located several hundred yards north of the Big Slide, you will see Ace of Spades and three other flows.

Directions: Park at the climber parking lot on the southbound side of Franconia Notch Parkway (I-93) and hike the bike path under the highway to the eastern side of the Notch. Walk one hundred feet north from the underpass and look for a wooded gully leading to Ace of Spades. Hike about a half mile up the gully to an avalanche scar and the ice climbing. Routes will be described from right to left as one approaches the flows from the gully.

★ Ace of Spades   II NEI 4

This is the best route here with an early season mixed start on the left and a more sustained direct variation via a pillar up the middle. Alternatively you can climb the original route up a steep first headwall to an ice cave, then move out right and up easier ice to the top. 150′

FA: Rainsford and Tim Rouner Winter 1974-75

Gareth Slattery leading a thin Ace Of Spades in late season   Jon Sykes

★ Overbid   II NEI 4+

Occasionally, just left of Ace of Spades, a 60-foot tall, free-standing pillar forms. This can be an arm pumping experience in thin conditions. The finish is the same as Trump Card.
FRA: Jose Abeyta and Dick Peterson December 14, 1980

Trump Card   II NEI 3

The start is ten feet left of Overbid up a ten-foot steep face.
At the top of the face move up a ramp past trees to the top.
FA: Rick Wilcox and Roger Martin Winter, 1976

Short Trick   II NEI 3

Fifty feet left (north) of Trump Card is another easy flow about 100 feet long with a twenty-foot headwall at the start and one final bulge at the top.
FWA: Jose Abeyta, Dick Peterson, and John Dedenski December 14, 1980

Ajilla Pospesil enjoying one of the many iceflows in the Big Slide area

Mike Lee

★ Big Slide

One of the more distinct features you will see on the eastern side of the notch is the huge avalanche scar just south of Ace of Spades. Big Slide has avalanched many times in the past one hundred years sending walls of mud, rocks, and trees into the highway. The slide offers multi-pitch ice climbs from grade 2 to 4. This is a great area for teaching French stepping.

Warning: Do not climb in this area if avalanche danger is present in the White Mountains.

The approach is the same as for Ace of Spades. Park at the climber parking lot and hike under the highway on the bike path. Walk south down the road a few hundred yards until below the slide. Hike in and take your pick.
FA: Unknown

Short Stack III NEI 4

This climb has one of the steeper approaches of any of the climbs in the Notch, and is a testament to the first ascentist's determination. Follow the major slide path up and right to the highest ice flow one can see from the road. Climb thin slab up to two 20-foot pillars, one on top of the other. A pumpy alpine gem.

FA: Chuck Woodman and Tim Smith February, 1995

Lafayette Ledges

Waist Deep and a Snowshoe Short III NEI 4 R

This climb has the longest approach of any of the ice in the Notch. Don't forget the snowshoes. Park at the Boise Rock parking lot, and hike into the woods at the East end of the parking lot; head up to the left end of the ledge system, about one mile. The climb starts on an iced-up slab (NEI 2) and climbs slabs for a hundred feet to four vertical tiers of ice. The first vertical section is the crux with thin ice, dry tooling, and no pro. The rest is fat ice to the top. Rap off trees to the right. The climb was done in one long pitch. 220'

FA: Jon Sykes and Mike Lee January 29, 1997

Lafayette Ledges ice climbing routes
1. Waist Deep and a Snowshoe Short NEI 4 R

Lonesome Lake

Up above Lonesome Lake on the south shoulder of Cannon Mountain are many icy slabs and icicles. This climb ascends the most prominent line on the right or east side of this collection of short climbs. Approach this area by desperate bushwacking up the hill from the packed trail at the east end of the lake. With luck, eventually you'll stumble upon this, or some other climb!

Leap of Faith   I NEI 3+

Scrape your way up an icy ramp for 40′ to a good stance below a steep, right-facing corner. Climb the corner on good ice, then make your way up steep but short headwalls to a belay in the bushes. Rappel the route with two ropes.

FA: Chuck Woodman and Michael Kennedy March, 1994

The author and his "Gypsy Mobile" after a long day "at work"   Chris Kratt

The author belays Val Michaud in The Flume   John Hession

The Flume Gorge

Located just south of the actual Notch, the Flume Gorge offers ice climbing from NEI Grade 3 to Grade 5 in a wonderful setting with easy top rope accessibility.

Access to the Gorge is via exit 33 off of the northbound lane of I-93. Follow the path around the left side of the Flume Visitors' Center for approximately one half mile crossing over a covered bridge and entering into the Gorge proper.

Important Notice: In the early season it is difficult to access ice climbs because the river may not be fully frozen. Exercise caution in approaching this climbing area. Also due to the cramped nature of the Gorge, never enter it without wearing a helmet.

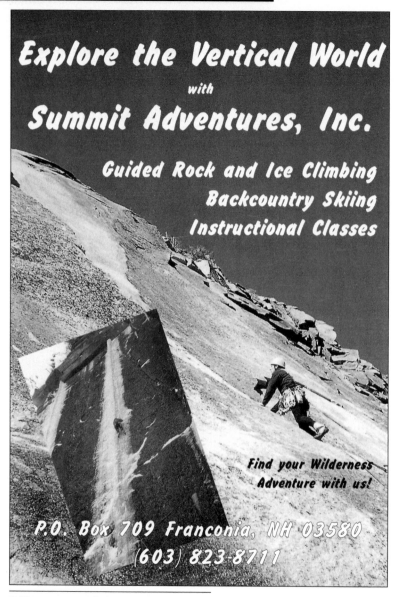

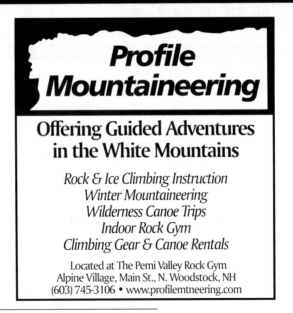

GEARED FOR THE VERTICAL WORLD

PETZL
ECRIN-ROC

PETZL
above
below
beyond

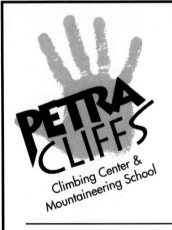

Index

The author leading the second pitch of the first ascent of Stone Fingers
Jamie Cunningham

About the Author

Jon Sykes has dedicated a better part of a decade exploring new and redis-covered territory in the western White Mountains, Maine and Vermont. Of the two hundred new routes that appear in this book, Jon has had a part in many of them. In fact, he has almost single-handedly developed whole areas with several supporting casts of characters. Many of his routes were accomplished rope solo from the ground up. It is largely due to his efforts that the climbing possibilities in the region have increased many fold. Cannon Cliff is no longer the sole destination for climbers—now there are whole new playgrounds of fun both on rock and ice!

Jon is a strong advocate of minimalist bolting and ground up first ascents. He is passionate about the stewardship, sportsmanship and ethic of his climbing, blending the traditional with the new. His bolted routes are not sporty clip-ups, but rather they keep challenge and commitment in the mix. A Sykes route is a route of conscious craftsmanship.

Jon had done much to maintain the trails, leading to both new and old areas, and is a founding member of The Friends of Franconia Notch. This is an organization set up by local climbers to insure stewardship of the trails and crags of this region. Jon's leadership and passion for climbing has brought many of his friends on a fantastic adventure here in the White Mountains. This adventure is now open for all to enjoy. Thank you, Jon!

Jon lives and works as an independent climbing guide out of Franconia New Hampshire.

Jamie Cunningham
Franconia, NH